D1443825

THE USBORNE COMPLETE BOOK OF M★A★G★I★C

Cheryl Evans and Ian Keable-Elliott

Designed by Jane Felstead

CONTENTS

Illustrated by Kim Raymond, Paul Sullivan, John Davey, Chris Lyon, Kim Blundell and Joseph McEwan.

ABOUT MAGIC

Magic is doing things that other people "know" are impossible. The art of the magician is to make it seem effortless and natural. People should be able to believe, if only for a short time, that you really have extraordinary powers.

The magicians in this picture are performing some of the different kinds of magic you will learn to do in this book.

Mentalism

Children's magic

Why do people like magic?

Despite the effects technology can achieve today, traditional magic is still very popular. Seeing an ordinary person do amazing things without the help of technology may be part of the appeal.

Magic is also a challenge. People are sure that if they concentrate hard enough they will be able to see how it is done.

Magicians are often funny and people enjoy laughing and being amazed at the same time. No matter what gets "lost" or "broken" during the act, it is all right in the end.

Magic is universal. Much magic does not require talking and can be appreciated worldwide.

How hard is it to learn?

You don't have to buy expensive equipment or be especially clever with your hands to do magic. There are tricks in this book that you will be able to do right away.

Others, though, do require special magic skills which are carefully explained and which you will need to learn and practice thoroughly. Gradually becoming more adept is part of the pleasure of doing magic.

Getting more from magic

If you are interested in magic, learning how to do it does not spoil the fun. Once you know some of its secrets you will understand the skill of experienced magicians and appreciate them even more.

What is in this book

The first 25 pages of this book tell you about different kinds of magic and introduce some of the terms and skills you need to know to perform tricks well. There are also practical examples for you to try.

Starting on page 30, there are masses of tricks of all kinds explained in detail, step-by-step. As far as possible, the tricks are shown as if you are looking at your own hands so the moves are easy to follow. Where it helps, what the audience should see is shown as well.

On pages 26-29 you can read about the history of magic and some of the most famous magicians.

A good way to use this book is to read some of the presentation techniques in the first half. Then turn to the tricks section and try to apply what you have learned to a specific trick. As you learn more tricks, keep referring back to the tips and hints on making them interesting and original.

Keeping the secret

Magicians have a sort of code of honor which means that they do not tell magic secrets to outsiders. This book is for people who really want to perform magic so don't tell anyone who is not a good magician how you do the tricks.

Learning more

This book provides you with the first steps to becoming a magician. You will become better by reading other books (you will find some suggestions on page 126) and by watching and meeting other magicians. Above all, you should start performing, as you will learn more from practical experience than any book or magician can teach you.

KINDS OF MAGIC

The type of tricks you want to do, where you perform and the kind of audience you perform to all determine what kind of magic you do. You may enjoy showing a few simple tricks to your family and friends or want to be a professional with a glittering stage show. Most magic falls into one of the categories shown here.

Children's magic

A magician may perform for young children at a party in their home, or in schools as well as in theatres. They usually use colorful equipment which appeals to children. Some may dress up, too. Young children love to join in, so the magician must enjoy working with them.

Magic for fun

Many people learn a few magic tricks just for their own fun. There are lots you can do without buying equipment, using household things such as playing cards, coins or matches. You can even carry these in your pockets and do tricks on the spot. There is one to try on the next page.

Close-up magic

Close-up magicians perform for a small audience, using things they carry in their pockets or a small case. You can easily do this sort of magic at home. Professionals may perform in restaurants, doing the same short act for different tables. They often chat and joke with the audience.

Silent magic

Magic is rarely done in total silence as most silent artistes work to music. The way they look is especially important, so they take great care over their costumes, equipment, gestures and expressions. The best silent acts are the most skilled of all magicians.

Cabaret magic

Cabaret, or stand-up, magic is the kind you most often see on stage or television. A cabaret is a theatre where people sit at tables to eat and watch a show afterwards. The acts are often funny, and some use elaborate equipment or have an assistant to add variety.

Illusions

Illusions are "impossible" feats with living things, such as making an elephant disappear. This usually requires large and expensive equipment so performers need to be quite well-established before they can afford to do them. They often have the help of assistants.

Escapology

Escapology involves escaping from all kinds of bonds and prisons. The performer must be fit and agile and have lots of nerve, as some escapes are really dangerous. It helps to be able to pick locks and untie knots but there are trick techniques that can help.

Mentalism

A mentalist does tricks that seem to be superhuman feats of the mind. They vary from predicting the future and reading people's minds to bending metal forks. The audience must believe that the mentalists' powers are real so their looks must be convincing.

Where's the Coin?

Try this trick at a table. All you need is a coin. Practice on your own first to make sure you can do it expertly. Unlike most tricks, this one can be repeated several times.

Do 2a and 2b at random as you repeat the trick.

Practice making the coin move fast, staying flat.

On a hard surface, the sound may give away which hand is hiding the coin. It works better on a tablecloth.

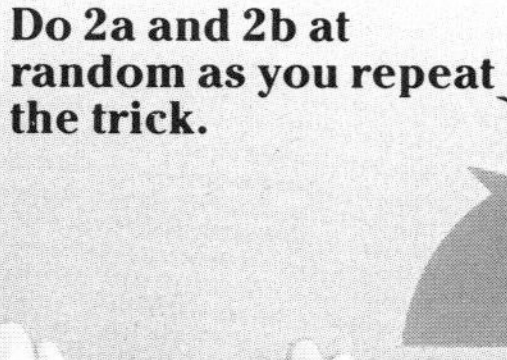

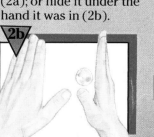

1 Put a coin in the palm of one hand. Place both hands flat on the table, palms-up.

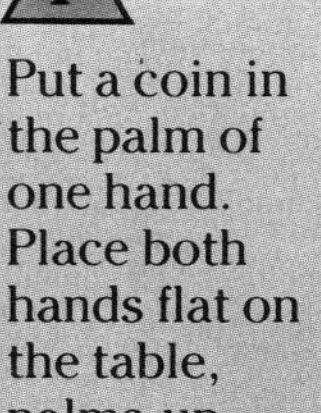

2a / 2b Turn your hands palms-down and either throw the coin under the other hand (2a); or hide it under the hand it was in (2b).

3 With your palms on the table and the coin covered ask people to guess which hand the coin is under.

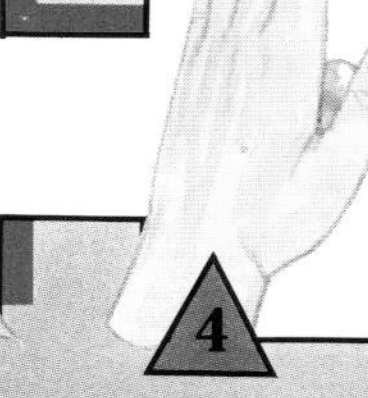

4 Turn over the hand they choose. They will often be wrong as 2a and 2b will look identical. Take the coin and start again.

PROPS

Whatever kind of magic you do, you need props (short for properties). Anything used during a performance is called a prop. You can find out about different types of props below, plus some tips for actually using them.

Types of props

Props vary from everyday things, such as a handkerchief, to specially bought or made equipment. You may use a prop simply to show your magic powers, by making it disappear, for example. Or the prop itself may make the magic work, such as a box with a false bottom. Props are also useful for attracting the audience's attention from secret moves.

Classic props

These are props that have been around for many years, but can be used in lots of fresh ways. The Linking Rings are one example. They link and come apart as the magician wishes.

Tricks for young children

These props are often brightly painted and feature themes that appeal to young children.

Traditional props

A top hat and wand are strongly linked with magic. Seeing them instantly tells people you are a magician.

Fakes and gimmicks

Fakes are familiar things that have been secretly altered. Gimmicks are props that are not seen, such as the servante in the picture.

Illusions

These are specially made props used by illusionists. They are expensive because you pay for the secret of how they work as much as for the equipment.

Live animals

Although you may occasionally see animals used in tricks, this can cause them accidental suffering as well as offending audiences. Don't imitate.

Tips on props

- *Mix special magic props with everyday things. People are often more amazed by magic done with familiar things than by strange gear.*

- *Be imaginative. Instead of a ball, use a small apple and hand it to someone after the trick. Or use a theme, such as Chinese props.*
- *Don't use too many props. If you can use the same one in several tricks, do so.*
- *Use appropriate props. A brightly colored box that is right for a children's act may not work in mentalism.*
- *Keep props in good condition. Wash and press silk scarves and re-paint boxes.*
- *Think about colors; blue props will not show against a blue shirt; lots of clashing colors look garish, for example.*

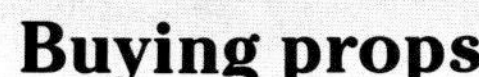

Magic Coin Spin

If you have a new, shiny coin, just spinning it as shown below will grab people's attention. This sort of eye-catching effect with a prop is called a flourish. Try it for yourself and when you can do it well, try the Magic Spin.

The flourish

Balance a coin on its rim on a table, with a flat side facing you. Rest your right first finger lightly on it to keep it upright. Flip your left first finger off your thumb to hit the flat face and make the coin spin. Lift your right finger as it starts.

The Magic Spin

Balance the coin as before. Stroke your left first finger along your right first finger a few times as if generating magic power. Have your left fingers curled, but stick your left thumb out underneath the finger balancing the coin.

Now stroke the left finger right off the end of the right, secretly flipping the coin with your left thumb to make it spin.

Buying props

You can buy props in magic shops, some toy departments, and direct from magic dealers. In shops, assistants will often show you how they work. They vary a lot in price but need not be very expensive. You can even make some yourself (see pages 58-59).

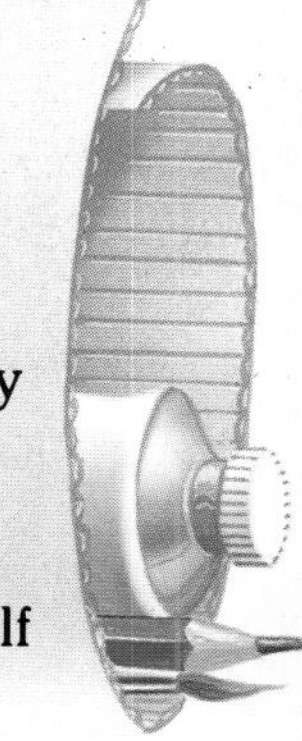

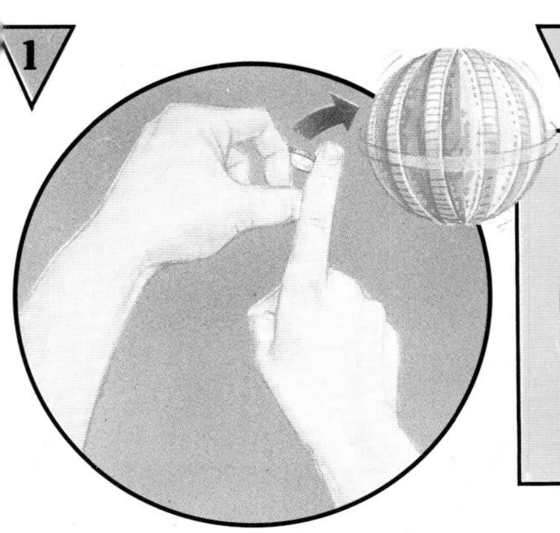

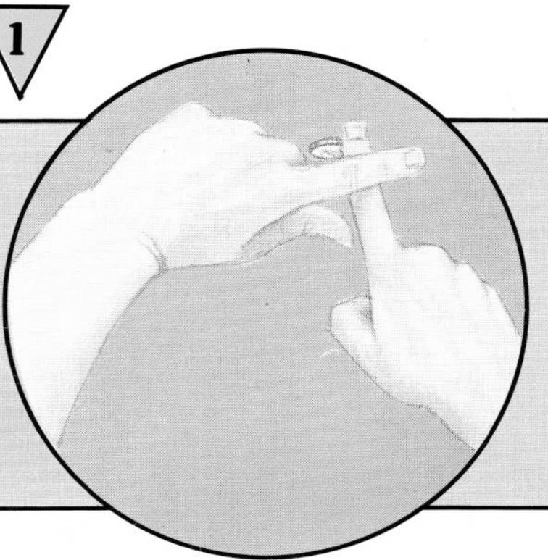

The audience does not see the flip. You seem to make the coin spin just by stroking.

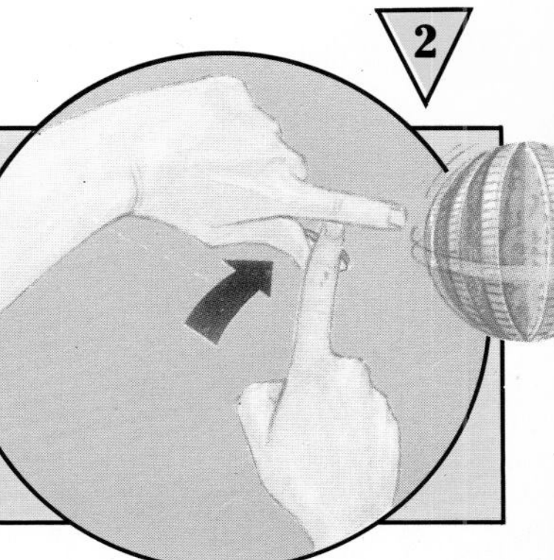

ACTING AND THE MAGICIAN

To be a good magician you do not have to pretend to be someone else, so don't worry if you think you cannot act. You do, however, need to think about how you look, speak and move during a performance. These are acting skills which you can find out about below.

Where you perform

The amount of acting you do can depend on where you perform. It may be appropriate to act an exaggerated character on a stage, but would seem silly for your friends and family at home. You also need to consider how many people are watching and how easily they can see.

On stage, playing a character can help entertain a large audience.

In close-up, a more natural style works better.

Acting tips

- *Try to relax and stand naturally. Don't shuffle or fidget.*
- *Your hands especially may be a problem. When not holding props, let them hang casually at your sides or hold them at waist level, with elbows bent.*
- *React to your tricks. Look surprised, pleased and so on. If you seem indifferent, the audience will be, too.*
- *Your body is expressive, too. You can raise your shoulders in exasperation or scratch your head in puzzlement.*
- *Prepare what you are going to say and speak clearly. Don't speak too fast. You can read more on this subject on pages 12-13.*
- *Watch magicians and other performers on television to see what they do and pick up hints.*

Slight of hand

Slight of hand is a name for secret moves in magic. Slights are necessary to make some tricks work and acting skills are vital to their success. This is a very useful slight, called the French Drop. You can also use it in the trick on the next page. Here it is shown from the audience's point of view.

Take a coin between your right thumb and first finger. Make sure everyone sees it.

Put your left hand over the coin as if to take it. Really, drop it onto your right fingers.

Your left hand hides what is happening.

Stagecraft

To make people feel part of the show, look directly at individuals as you talk to them.

◀ Don't turn your back on people. They soon get bored if they cannot see your face or hear you speak. To move backwards, cross the stage diagonally or simply step back.

Walk behind things ▶ you want seen, such as a prop or assistant. You can walk in front if what you are saying or doing is more important than anything else.

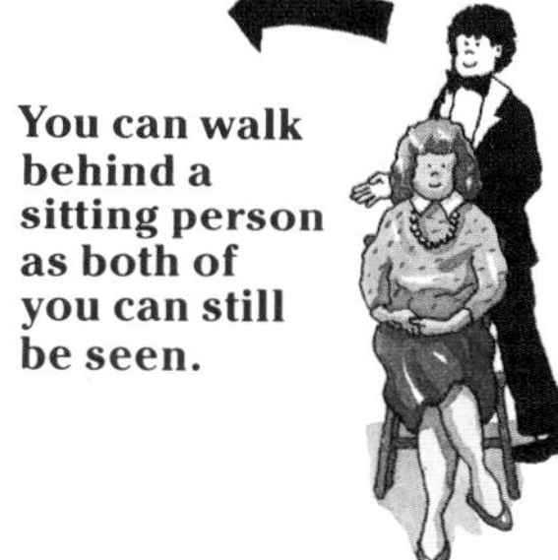

You can walk behind a sitting person as both of you can still be seen.

With these two silk hankies . . .

◀ It is hard for the audience to watch your face, listen and see what you are doing all at once. Try to avoid this unless you want to misdirect (see pages 10-11).

A name to conjure with

If you like, you can use a different name when you do magic. Some magicians like to invent one to suit their act: a funny one or a mock title such as "Professor" or a mysterious foreign name, for example.

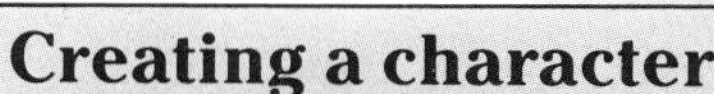

Creating a character

Acting helps create a stage "persona". This is a character you may become when performing. A well-chosen and developed persona can improve your performance. It usually evolves over years of experience; don't try to force one on yourself.

This is the English magician, Tommy Cooper. He was a good magician, but seeming incompetent was part of his persona.

Close your left hand and move it away as if it has the coin. Follow it with your eyes.

3
Keep your right hand still.

Turn your left hand over, watching it with interest Let the right hand drop naturally.

4

Uncurl your left hand. Act amazed that the coin has gone and the audience will be, too.

5

Later, when the trick is over, put your right hand in your pocket and leave the coin there.

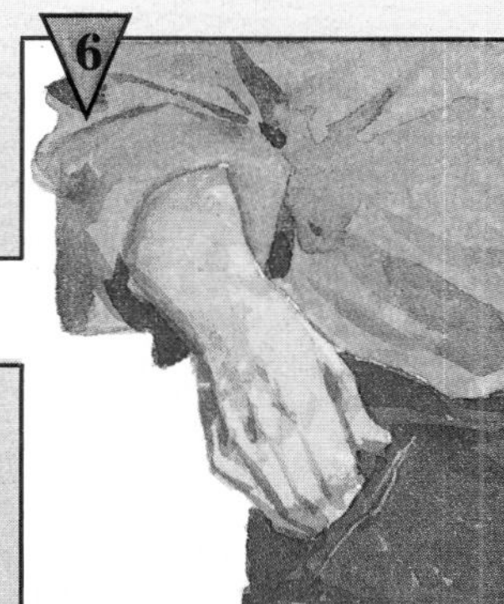
6

MISDIRECTION

Misdirection is a subtle skill used to hide secret moves. It takes thought and practice. The Coin Vanish trick at the bottom of the page uses the French Drop slight from the last page and some subtle misdirection.

Ways to misdirect

It may seem hard to hide things from an audience that is watching closely. In fact, it is quite easy to deceive them. Some ways are given here. Several may apply at once and work together to misdirect.

Eye foolers

People's eyes tell them things that may not be true. If you seem to swap a coin from one hand to the other convincingly, they believe what they think they have seen.

Attracting attention

If you draw attention to a prop in one hand, something hidden in the other will go unnoticed.

Allaying suspicions

Audiences are suspicious. They try to spot how tricks are done. To combat this, handle props casually and openly so there does not seem to be anything to hide. Let the audience examine some of them.

Using repetition

If you do the same thing again and again, the audience stops watching closely. You could shuffle cards in the same way several times before doing a slight with the same shuffle.

Where to look

Look directly at the audience and they will tend to look at your face; look at a prop or your hand, and they look at those.

The psychological moment

There are times when an audience is less alert, such as when a trick is just over. They don't expect more magic yet. If you do a slight then, it is less likely to be seen.

Big versus small

A big noise or gesture hides a smaller one. Plan to make a deliberate loud noise part of your act to hide a slight that makes a little noise, such as a coin clinking.

Time lapse

Memories are short, especially if lots is going on. If you are left with a prop hidden in your hand, wait a bit so people forget. Then get rid of it.

Coin Vanish

Place a coin and wand (or use a pencil) on a table. Take the coin in your right hand and show it to the audience.

Look at the wand as if you want to pick it up but cannot because of the coin. This creates a reason to do the next step.

2
People look where you look, not at your hands.

Pretend to swap the coin to your left hand, but really French Drop it into your right. Keep looking at the wand.

Tips on misdirection

- *Don't rely on slights being perfect; use misdirection as well, to be sure.*
- *Always invent a good reason for doing something. If you want to take something secretly from your pocket, do it when you are openly putting something away.*
- *Match your misdirection to your style. If your act is low key, a sudden shout or gesture would seem out of place. A wry joke or amusing expression might be more suitable.*

Misdirection or distraction?

You can easily distract people for a moment by exclaiming and pointing at the ceiling. This is not misdirection. The audience would know it had been tricked and would not be fooled more than once or twice.

Misdirection in close-up

You may think that misdirection is trickier when the audience is close to you. In fact, it is hard for them to focus on more than a small part of you at once. Here's how you can make use of this:

Find out people's names and use them. They will look up at your face and away from your hands.

Ask people to help, by shuffling cards, perhaps. Other spectators will watch them, diverting attention from you.

From this close, the spectator cannot watch your face and hands at the same time.

Misdirection on stage

When you are on stage, people can see everything you do at a glance. You may need to use bigger gestures to misdirect. Here are some other techniques that help:

Spectator can take all of you in at the same time.

Using volunteers from the audience or having an assistant on stage takes attention away from you.

What you say misdirects. You can lead the audience to expect one thing, so they are surprised when something else happens.

Pick up the wand with your right hand, too. Now turn your attention to your left fist, where the coin is meant to be.

Tap your left fist with the wand as if working magic. (Really, the magic was in step 3. This time delay helps to misdirect.)

Uncurl your hand slowly, watching with interest. React with surprise or delight that the coin has gone.

Audience responds to your reaction.

PATTER

Patter is the name for what you say during an act. It should sound natural but, in fact, a lot of work goes into making it informative and amusing.

What to say

Build a framework of patter around things you must say, such as introducing yourself, greeting the audience, explaining what they need to know and linking tricks.

Pitfalls to avoid

Here are some examples of things not to say:

Stating the obvious

I am now picking up this handkerchief.

The audience can see what you are doing. You don't need to say it as well.

Arousing suspicions

I put it in this envelope, which is quite standard and has not been tampered with in any way.

You would not expect there to be anything odd about an envelope. Stating it may put ideas into people's heads.

Spoiling the surprise

And when I pull it out again it will have turned green.

As a general rule, avoid anticipating the effect by what you say.

Making it more interesting

As you get more confident, you can expand and improve your patter with some of the following ideas:

Storytelling

You could tell the history of a ▶ trick if it has an interesting origin. Or make up a story in which the magic becomes part of the action. Be careful not to make the story too long or the audience may get bored.

This rope trick is said to be a very old Indian effect.

Fantasy

◀ Particularly for acts or tricks involving mentalism or mind-reading, you can suggest that the tricks are done by the power of the mind or with the assistance of unknown forces.

Humour

It is quite hard to be funny, ▶ but here are some tips:

Make jokes relevant. A gag that is unrelated to the trick is simply distracting.

Keep it short. What comedians call "one-liners" work well. These are short, funny asides dropped into your speech.

Work on your timing. This means choosing the moment to tell a joke, pausing before the punchline for impact and allowing time for laughter afterwards. You can only learn timing by experience.

I keep going to pieces today.

Tips on talking

- *In close-up magic use your normal voice. On a stage you may need to talk more slowly and clearly than usual. If there is a microphone (see below), speak normally.*
- *Talk naturally. Don't worry about your accent. It can be part of your persona (see page 9). As long as you talk clearly, people will understand.*
- *Cut out annoying speech habits, such as "you know" and "sort of" and using clichés. If you don't think you do any of these, ask a friend to listen to you and criticize.*
- *Use patter to create drama. Talk gradually more slowly to show concentration and build up suspense, for instance. Talk louder and faster at the climax.*

Patter should not be repeated parrot-fashion. Aim to make it sound fresh and natural, even when you say it for the hundredth time.

Using microphones

There is no need to shout.

A microphone amplifies your voice so it can be heard by everyone. You talk quite normally. The most important thing for performers is that their hands are free to handle props while they are speaking. Nowadays, clip-on microphones can be attached to a lapel or hung around your neck.

Patter to avoid

Insulting the audience. Some professional magicians get away with this, but you cannot expect to.

Jokes about people's race or sex or issues they may feel deeply about such as religion or politics.

Illogical patter, such as a very young magician referring to "my wife".

Too many puns, except for children, as they love bad puns.

"Dirty" or "blue" jokes.

Other people's patter. Someone else's lines will not sound so good when you say them and audiences will not be impressed by your lack of originality.

Rehearsed patter

You may find it quite hard at first to manipulate props and talk at the same time, so be sure to rehearse both together.

Ad-libs

Ad-libs are unrehearsed comments that occur to you. They can put you off your stride if you are not careful. If you like you can prepare "ad-lib" lines and use them if the chance arises. These are not true ad-libs but still work if they seem spontaneous.

Looking for patter

Here are some places to look for ideas for patter:

Books about magic for the history of tricks. (There are some suggested titles on page 62.)

Look out for odd stories in the newspapers.

Joke books, comics, television or funny things your friends say.

Keep a notebook of things you want to remember.

SILENT ACTS

Not all magicians use patter. Some illusionists perform silently to dramatic music, for instance. To magicians, a silent act usually means one performed to music, involving tricks using more manipulation skills than in a patter act. Below you can see some of the ways a silent act differs from a patter act.

You cannot get your personality across by words, so you must be interesting to look at. Costume and gestures show your persona.

You have to do more magic as there are no jokes or stories to help entertain. Magic must happen continuously.

Your slight of hand must be excellent and your misdirection convincing, as you have no other means to divert attention.

You can less afford to make mistakes as it is harder to bluff your way out. You must rehearse even more than other magicians.

Silent artistes sometimes use other skills such as mime or dance to help entertain during their act.

All aspects of the show must be as perfect as possible. People notice clothes, music and props more if there is no patter to listen to.

The act may be quite short since it demands a lot of audience concentration, which can only be maintained for short periods.

A good silent act is probably the hardest to do well but, if you succeed, it can be performed anywhere in the world.

Choosing and using music

Use a variety of music, making sure the different pieces flow smoothly from one to the next. As a guide, use cheerful music for your entrance, gentle tunes to relax the audience and something exciting for a climax. Don't choose a recent hit record or it will soon seem dated. Record your choices on a cassette and always rehearse to it. It is crucial to tie music and tricks together. A certain sequence of tricks must coincide exactly with a specific piece of music.

COSTUME

You don't have to have special clothes to do magic. You can perform in casual gear, but most people performing for an audience feel they want to dress the part. What you wear depends on the show you do and impression you want to make.

What to wear

A good general rule is to wear something smarter than your audience. As most magic is performed at a special night out or party, the kind of clothes these magicians have on should be suitable.

Labels round the picture show some important points about clothes for magicians. You might wear something very different for street performing, say, or to create a persona.

Jacket has plenty of pockets, inside and outside, which a magician can use.

Smart trousers also have back and side pockets.

Make sure shoes are clean and socks match. People will focus on anything odd or scruffy.

Silk scarf in hair can be taken out and used in tricks.

Secret pockets can be hidden in folds and belts.

Jewellery, fake flowers and so on can be used as props.

A bag is a good place to carry props.

Other styles

Some magicians wear a bright or glittery costume. These are specially made and cost a lot.

A traditional black tailcoat is elegant and versatile. Hat, gloves and wand are useful accessories.

Character costumes may be worn in a pantomime or play. This magician is dressed as a wizard.

Doctored costumes

Some people think magicians have lots of secret pockets and other hiding places. In fact, they mostly use existing pockets and natural hiding places in a lapel or belt. Special devices are sometimes used, though:

This is a bag holder. It opens at the bottom to let a prop drop into your hand.

This small pocket on the outside of a costume is a dip pocket. It is in matching cloth, at arm's length.

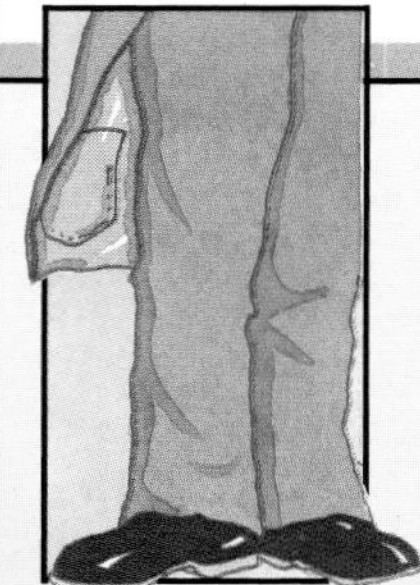

A pocket inside a jacket or under a coat tail, like this, is a toppit.

Where to get costumes

Rent them from a theatrical costumier or fancy dress shop. Find them in your phone book.

Evening wear rent shops often have sales of used stock.

Search in junk shops for second-hand evening clothes, accessories and props.

If you are good at sewing you could make your own.

Before you do a trick you must rehearse it thoroughly. It takes a lot of practice to get the movements perfect and think of an interesting presentation. Read about ways to rehearse below then try them out on the trick at the bottom of the page.

Practicing slights

Follow the pink arrow and instructions to rehearse this Finger Palm slight. Practice in a mirror to make sure it looks natural. Once you feel confident, stop using the mirror and try not to look at your hands. Most slights can be used in many tricks.

The pictures in circles show what you see in the mirror.

In the mirror, the real move and slight should look the same.

Move this hand away.

Slight.

Keep this hand still.

Real move.

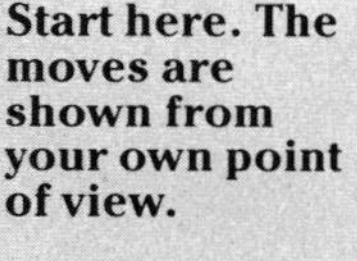

Start here. The moves are shown from your own point of view.

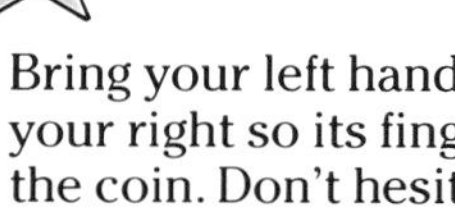

Practice the real move first, then do the slight to look the same.

1. Hold up the coin between the thumb and first two fingers of your right hand. Do it quite casually.

2. Bring your left hand over your right so its fingers hide the coin. Don't hesitate, but carry smoothly on to the next step.

3. First, take the coin and move your left hand away. For the slight, pretend to do the same, but actually drop the coin onto your right fingers.

Coin Through a Handkerchief

To rehearse this trick, practice the slight on its own first, as shown above. Then work on the other aspects involved in making a trick successful, such as patter, misdirecting the audience and linking the trick to those that come before and after. To do it you need a coin and a handkerchief.

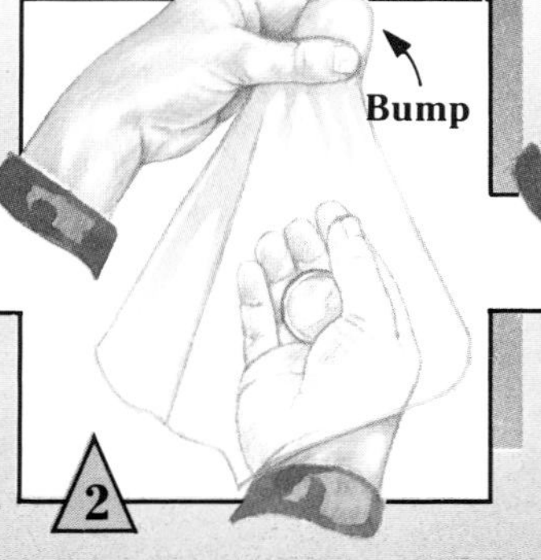

1. Hold up the coin in your right hand. With your left hand, drape a handkerchief over it. There is a bump where the coin is.

2. Take the bump with your left hand. People think this is the coin. In fact, use the slight above to drop the coin into your right fingers.

3. Lift the handkerchief off your right hand, still gripping the bump. You leave the coin in your right hand.

How to rehearse a trick

Here are some steps to take when thinking about how to perform a trick. The magician on the right points out how to apply some of them to the trick at the bottom of the page.

You need a handkerchief that will keep the shape of the coin even when it is not really there. Crisp linen is better than silk.

Work on individual slights.

Familiarize yourself with the props and make sure they work.

Try to spot weak points, when people may see how the trick is done. Decide how to misdirect.

Step 5 is a danger spot. Talk, so people don't look at your hands.

Work out what to say from start to finish.

Work out how you will link tricks.

Perform the trick right through several times.

Rehearsal tips

- *You can always improve a trick. Keep working on it.*
- *Wear the clothes you will wear on stage.*
- *Perfect a small number of tricks rather than do a lot sloppily.*
- *Treat the first time you do a new trick as another rehearsal. You cannot know if it works until you perform for real.*
- *Rehearse frequently but in small doses. You are more likely to overcome a problem when you come to it fresh.*
- *Try a new trick on friends or family and listen to their criticisms. If you have access to a video, film yourself and criticize your performance.*

Stage fright

Stage fright is an attack of nerves on stage. You forget what you are saying and make mistakes. Thorough rehearsal reduces the risk of it. Being scared before you start is anticipation not stage fright.

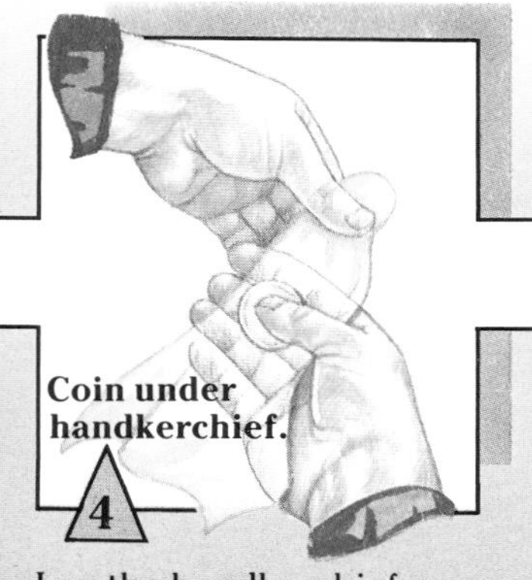

Lay the handkerchief on your right palm, on top of the coin that is hidden there. The audience still thinks the bump is where the coin is.

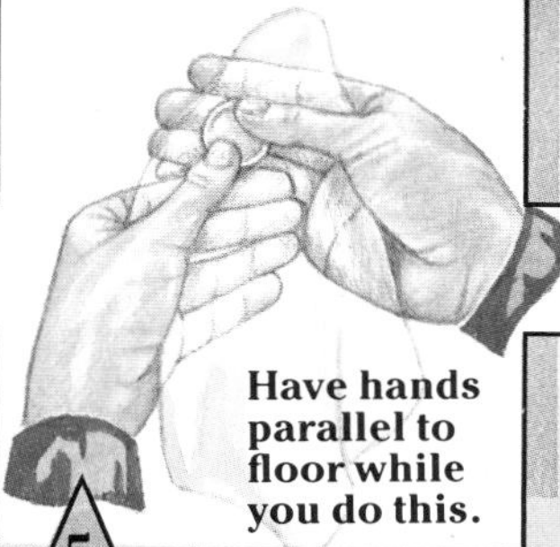

Have hands parallel to floor while you do this.
5

Pass your left hand back towards you close underneath your right hand, taking the coin from your right hand with your left.

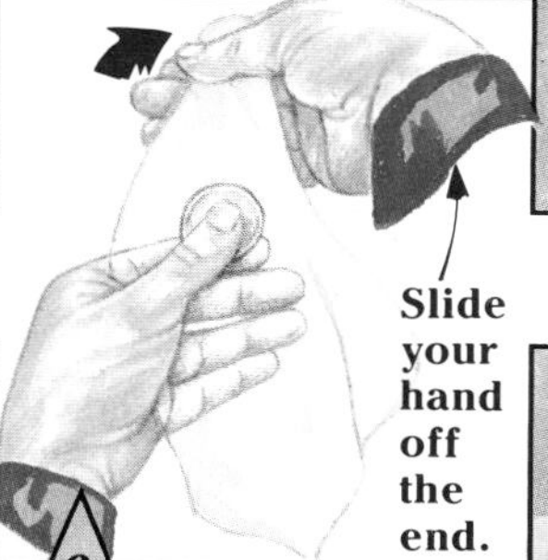

Slide your hand off the end.
6

Grip the handkerchief with your left hand. Pretend to try and squeeze the coin out through the end of it with your right hand.

Coin appears here.

Under the handkerchief, take the coin from your left hand with your right fingers. Let it emerge from the bump as if through the material.

ASSISTANTS, VOLUNTEERS AND STOOGES

Many magicians use helpers. They may be trained assistants who always rehearse and work with them. Or they can be volunteers from the audience. The trick on the page opposite depends on another kind of helper called a stooge that you can find out about below. You will need to teach a friend to do it with you.

Assistants

Some assistants are unobtrusive. They hand things to the performer and quietly remove props that are finished with, for example. They dress discreetly and are hardly noticed by the audience.

Others play a more active role. They may display props, take part in tricks, provide misdirection or even pretend to be clumsy or incompetent for a funny effect.

Stooges

A stooge is someone from the audience posing as a volunteer. The magician tells him before the show what to do and say to make the trick work. It can be a problem for the helper to act naturally so no-one else suspects he is a stooge.

Some professionals can make genuine volunteers act as stooges by telling them secretly what to do once up on stage. Most people will be prepared to go along with it, but it is risky.

Volunteers and how to choose them

Volunteers are picked from the audience to watch or to help. It is quite often hard to see and judge spectators to choose a good volunteer. If possible (for instance in close-up magic), chat to the audience before the show.

If the lighting makes seeing difficult, walk out among the audience for a better look.

Volunteers should seem to be chosen randomly, but here are some things to look out for to find good ones:

A person whose looks contrast with yours.

People obviously having fun.

Reactions that might add to the effect, such as giggles.

Someone to reinforce an impression: a big man to test the strength of a prop, say.

Someone from a large group; their family or friends will egg them on.

For real randomness, throw something easy to catch, such as a ping-pong ball, and ask whoever catches it.

Tips on volunteers

- *People who choose to sit near the front are usually quite keen to volunteer.*
- *Make sure they will have no physical difficulty helping.*
- *Treat them well, thank them and ask for applause. See them safely back off stage.*
- *Give clear instructions.*
- *Use them in the middle of an act. They can be distracting during your first trick or when taking your final bow.*
- *Don't use them for the sake of it. What they do must enhance the act.*

Coin Vanish with Handkerchief

This trick is a version of the trick on pages 16-17. To perform it, you need a stooge. He or she must keep a straight face and not give anything away. Rehearse together thoroughly. In these pictures you see what the audience sees.

1 Hold the coin up and show it to the audience. Then cover it with a handkerchief, as in the previous trick.

2 Take hold of the coin and the handkerchief with your left hand, and lift them both off your right hand.

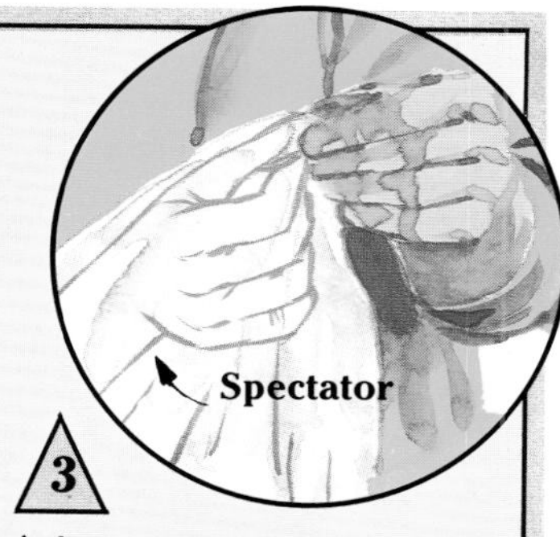

3 Ask a spectator to feel the coin. Insist his hand goes under the handkerchief. Repeat with other spectators.

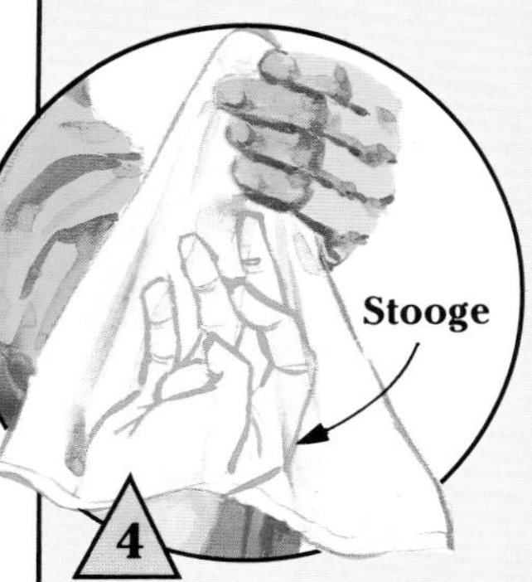

4 Now ask the stooge and let him take the coin when he withdraws his hand. If he can Finger Palm it, he should.

5 Go through steps 4 and 5 of the trick on page 17, ignoring the coin because you no longer have it. This is good time misdirection; it separates the moment when the trick took place (when the stooge took the coin) from the revelation that the coin has gone. People forget who last touched the coin under the handkerchief and do not think it is important, anyway.

6 This step is the same as step 6 on page 17 only, as you stroke, look puzzled that the coin does not appear.

7 Finally, give up and shake out the handkerchief to show that the coin has completely vanished.

Advantages of using helpers

Many tricks cannot be performed without help, so using assistants and volunteers increases the range of tricks you can do.

Using volunteers involves the audience so the act is more interesting to them.

An enthusiastic assistant will give help and support and may be able to make useful suggestions for improving the act

Jokes and chat with helpers provide variety and help fill out the act.

Disadvantages of using helpers

Assistants work as hard as magicians, without much credit. They may get fed up and leave to follow their own career.

Getting people to volunteer can be difficult and may embarrass the audience.

Volunteers can spoil a trick, accidentally or even on purpose.

Working professionally, it is hard to get twice as much money as on your own, but you must still pay your helper.

WHEN THINGS GO WRONG

Every "live" performer dreads something going wrong and, in magic, the risk is quite high. Thorough rehearsal should prevent most mistakes but unforeseen problems will still arise. The information on these two pages will help you avoid or deal with tricky situations, but only experience can really make you confident.

About your audience

At first, it is easy to feel that the audience is just waiting for you to do something wrong. In fact, people are not nearly as critical as you think and are really on your side. Try to remember these points:

People would rather be entertained than simply fooled. As long as they enjoy the show they will not worry if they see how a trick is done or detect a slight.

Most people realize and respect how hard magic is. If a trick fails, they feel sympathy. Don't embarrass them by getting flustered and over-apologizing, and they will probably warm to you all the more.

People have very short memories. They are more likely to remember your successful tricks than mistakes.

You are very conscious of mistakes, but an audience may not even notice them.

Avoiding problems with props

Make a check list of where your props should be at the start of the act. Use it each time you set up. Always check that props work just before you perform, even if they worked fine the last time you used them.

Avoiding problems with people

Would you stand over here, please?

It is up to you to ensure that volunteers do what you want them to.

You want that one? Let's be difficult and use this one, then.

Avoid asking questions if the wrong answer could spoil your trick.

Yes, well . . .thank you for your help . . .

If a volunteer ruins a trick abandon it and get him politely off stage.

Tips on coping

Here are some ideas that could prevent disaster when you make a mistake:

- *You may be able to change the ending by doing a different magic effect. The audience doesn't know what you had planned, so they will not even notice.*
- *Start again, if your mistake has not revealed any secrets. Tell the audience what you are doing. They will think the trick must be difficult and be all the more impressed when you succeed.*
- *If all else fails, move on to a new trick. Joke about it if you can. If you are not uneasy, others will not be.*

More serious problems

If your whole act goes down badly, it may be for one of the reasons below. There are suggestions to help solve the problems, too.

Problem: You genuinely do not perform the act well on one particular evening.

Solution: Try to develop a routine to help key yourself up and prepare for each performance.

Problem: The audience is not in a receptive mood. This may be because they have other distractions, such as food (in a restaurant) or dancing and chatting (at a party).

Solution: All you can do is perform to the best of your ability and hope to catch one or two people's attention. Once a few people start to watch, others usually follow through curiosity.

Problem: The act may not be suitable for that particular audience.

Solution: Try to find out what sort of audience to expect where you are performing. The same act can be made to suit different audiences by a subtle change of patter or presentation.

"Dying" on stage

When a whole act is badly received it is called "dying". If the audience is clearly not watching or starts to make critical comments, you know something is seriously wrong. It is better to struggle on rather than stopping, for these reasons:

You may do a trick later which people like so you win back their attention.

You will find out far more about your act, and what is wrong with it, by performing to the end.

People like performers who don't give in. You may gain their respect, at least, if you keep trying.

Coin Recovery

Here you can see how a mistake can be made into part of the act. If you accidentally drop a coin while doing the French Drop, say, you could pick it up and try again but the audience may have seen it fall from the "wrong" hand and realize how the slight is done. Instead, try this trick.

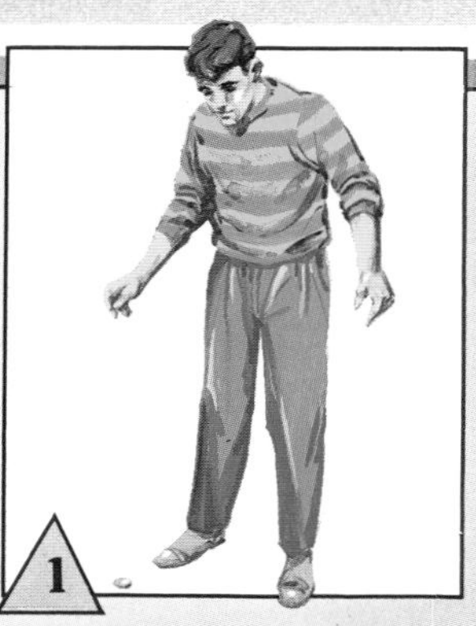

1 Place one foot near the coin on the floor. If you need to get nearer to it, move around as though looking for it.

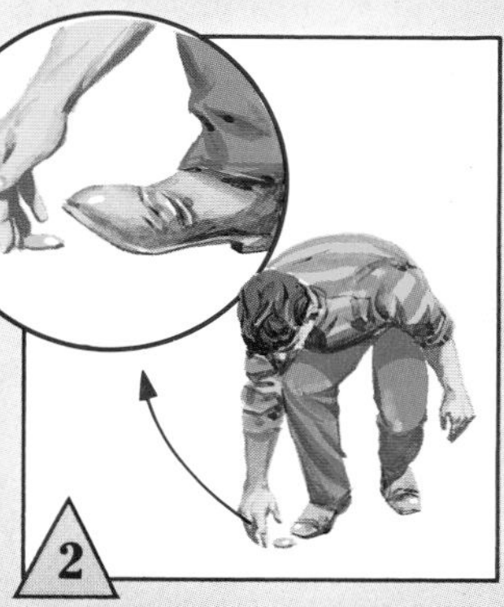

2 Bend down to pick up the coin but, actually, lift your toe and slide the coin under it as you close your hand.

3 Stand up and say you will try again. Pretend to put the coin into the other hand.

4 With a magic gesture, open the hand that is meant to have the coin in it, then the other. The coin has vanished.

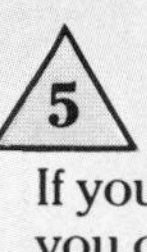

5 If you have a spare coin you can now carry on as you originally intended. Or move on to another trick. Although this leaves you with your foot on the coin so you cannot move around, don't try to pick it up too soon. You could do another trick in which a coin vanishes and "appears" under your foot. Or deliberately let something else drop and pick up the coin at the same time.

PLANNING AN ACT

Magicians usually plan a linked series of tricks to form an act. You can build an act gradually from tricks that you like doing and perform well. Rather than just letting it grow haphazardly, though, it is a good idea to think honestly about your own strengths and weaknesses and the kind of audience you expect to perform for. You can then use the tips below to help work out a balanced performance.

Things to consider when planning an act

If you find it easy to chat to all kinds of people you will probably enjoy doing a patter act. You will get more personal contact in close-up work than a stage act.

If you are good at telling jokes and being funny, plan a comedy act. If not, don't force it. You might try to amaze the audience with your dexterity, elegance or dramatic effects instead.

Experiment with different styles to discover the one you enjoy most. If you enjoy yourself, the audience should, too.

If you want to do a silent act, you might feel you could benefit from mime or acting lessons.

It is a golden rule of magic only to work with young children if you genuinely enjoy it.

Shaping an act

This curved orange path shows the ideal shape of an act. Read how to include pace and variety by starting at the Opening, below, and following the path to the Finish on the next page. The basic shape is the same whatever your act.

On the notepads are tricks from this book which fit in the places shown.

Close-up:
Instant Revelation
Pegasus

Children's:
Hello Routine

Cabaret:
Cut and Restored Rope

Silent:
Miser's Dream

Upward curves show where exciting things happen.

Downward curves show quieter moments. They are necessary to provide contrast and give the audience a chance to relax.

The Opening

First impressions are vital so start with something short but exciting. Let the audience get to know you. Don't introduce an assistant or use a volunteer yet.

Intersperse a few short effects between longer, more complex tricks to link and provide variety.

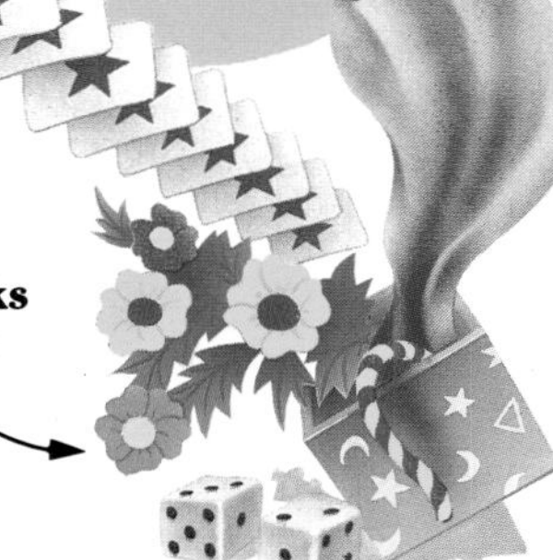

The Middle

Do longer tricks here. If you have people's attention, they will not mind waiting a bit for a good climax. Use an assistant for variety. The audience should be relaxed now, so it is a good time to ask for volunteers, too.

Cabaret:
Glasses and Bottles
Escapology:
Sack Escape
Children's:
Toy Rabbit Production
Mentalism:
Newspaper Prediction

Close-up:
Do As I Do
Copper and Silver
Cabaret:
Coin in Wool
Two Card Trick
Children's:
Farmyard Noises

The general trend of the act is upwards. Quieter moments should not let interest drop back to the level before the previous peak.

The Finish

Save your most spectacular trick for last. Producing something is better than making it vanish as people can see and applaud it. Don't use helpers here, so you can take your final bow alone.

Lengths of acts

It is impossible to say how long an act should be as they vary so much. There are basic differences between the average lengths of different sorts of act, though, as this table shows.

Type of magic	Time in minutes	Comments
Close-up	5-10	You will probably be expected to repeat the act several times to different groups of people over a period of 1 to 3 hours.
Cabaret	20-45	To keep the audience entertained for this length of time, cabaret acts usually involve plenty of humour.
Silent	10	Silent acts tend to be shorter because magic is happening all the time, which requires a lot of concentration from the audience and magician.
Children's	30-60	Children need plenty of variety and excitement to hold their attention. Doing magic for children can be exhausting.
Illusions Mentalism Escapology	5-60	A full-length show in these styles might last an hour but a magician may also do just one trick in a variety show.

Audiences rarely complain that an act is too short. It's a good idea to leave them wanting more.

It is very hard to be a professional magician. The best preparation is to get as much performing experience as you can.

Many magicians start as semi-professionals, which means doing magic while still holding an ordinary job.

Getting started

It is worth doing any magic work so that people get to know you. Your reputation will spread mainly by word of mouth at first. You could get a card printed to give to anyone who shows an interest in you.

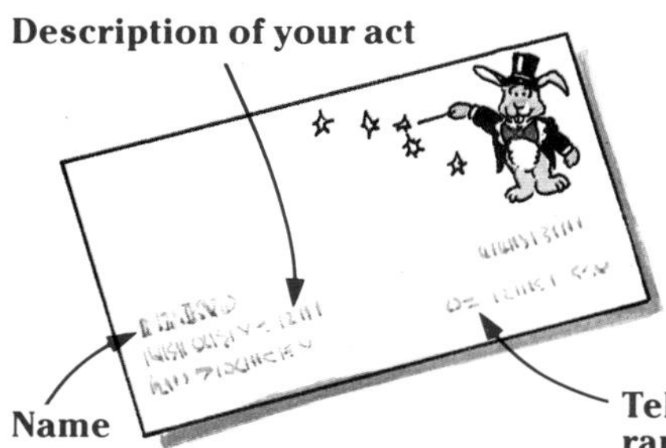

For wider publicity, ask a local paper to send a reporter to see you. Enclose a ticket and mention that you are a new, young magicians.

Opportunities to perform

Finding places to perform takes a lot of effort. There are more opportunities to perform some kinds of magic than others. Here are some suggestions:

Hospitals and homes

Offer to perform for your local hospital, children's or retirement home. They are unlikely to be able to pay, though you might get expenses. Try to contact someone in charge of entertainments.

Parties

Magicians can usually find plenty of work at children's parties and sometimes at adults' parties, too. People look for a magician in their area, so an advertisement in the local telephone directory or paper could be useful.

Charities

A local charity might help you organize a show and sell tickets if you perform to raise money for their funds. Call or write and suggest it.

Cruises

Some cruise operators book cabaret acts for an evening, one trip or a whole season.

Talent contests

Talent contests are held to find good new acts. You compete against other acts such as singers or comedians, and it is good experience. Contests are advertised in newspapers or locally. You may have to travel to your nearest big town to attend.

Hotels and restaurants

Close-up and cabaret work may be found in hotels and restaurants. See if the owner or manager is interested.

Magic for businesses

A company may employ a magician to promote products at trade shows or business parties. Try approaching a suitable firm's Public Relations officer.

Street performing

Vacation places often allow street entertaining. Check with the police whether you need permission.

Discos

Magic in discos is becoming popular. Your act must work against a background of disco music and lights.

Theatres and cabarets

For most theatre or cabaret work you need an agent (see next page). For experience, ask an amateur drama group if they could use you in a play.

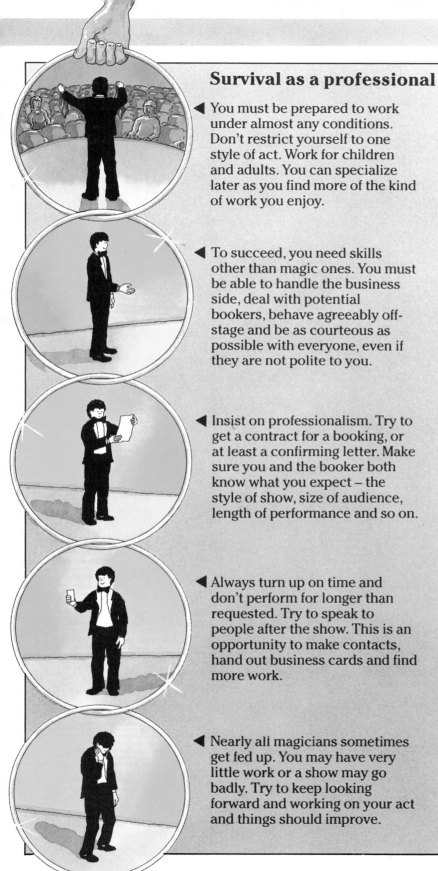

Survival as a professional

◀ You must be prepared to work under almost any conditions. Don't restrict yourself to one style of act. Work for children and adults. You can specialize later as you find more of the kind of work you enjoy.

◀ To succeed, you need skills other than magic ones. You must be able to handle the business side, deal with potential bookers, behave agreeably off-stage and be as courteous as possible with everyone, even if they are not polite to you.

◀ Insist on professionalism. Try to get a contract for a booking, or at least a confirming letter. Make sure you and the booker both know what you expect – the style of show, size of audience, length of performance and so on.

◀ Always turn up on time and don't perform for longer than requested. Try to speak to people after the show. This is an opportunity to make contacts, hand out business cards and find more work.

◀ Nearly all magicians sometimes get fed up. You may have very little work or a show may go badly. Try to keep looking forward and working on your act and things should improve.

Asking for money

If you want to make a living from magic you must charge for it. The amount depends on the kind of act, the venue and your experience.

Find out what people with a similar act charge and ask the same. Don't take a much reduced fee as this undermines other professional magicians.

Agents

An agent is someone to whom people apply to book an act. If your name is on an agent's list, it will be put forward for suitable work.

You pay a percentage of your fee for this service. You can ask an agent to take you on but he will want to see your act and decide for himself.

Managers

A manager promotes you and goes out looking for work for you. He or she usually demands a high salary or percentage of your earnings. A manager will only offer to take you on if you have the potential to earn a lot.

THE STORY OF MAGIC

From ancient times

Magic has probably been used from the earliest times by witch doctors and other wonder workers.

In Ancient Greece and Rome, priests used magic to produce "miraculous" effects during religious ceremonies. Secret mechanisms could make temple doors open by themselves or wine flow from statues.

The earliest records

The oldest written record of a magic performance is in an Egyptian scroll dated about 2600 BC. It tells of an illusionist called Dedi entertaining the Pharaoh, Cheops.

In the first century AD, a Roman called Seneca wrote about seeing a magician. He described the cup and balls trick, in which balls appear and disappear under three upturned beakers. It is still widely performed today.

Dangerous times

In Medieval Europe, magic was confused with witchcraft, which was punishable by death. In 1584, an Englishman called Reginald Scot wrote a book called *The Discoverie of Witchcraft*. It showed how some slights were done to prove that it was not with the help of the Devil.

Travelling showmen

For a long time, magic was not respectable. In the 16th century, magicians travelled around performing where they could. They often set up booths at fairs and markets.

Novelties, such as stone-swallowing, were popular, as well as conventional magic. From the late 16th century, there were many "intelligent" animal acts. A man called Banks and his horse, Marocco, were a great success in London in the 1580s, for example.

Marocco counted by tapping his hoof and could identify people in the audience from a description of them.

Fashions in magic

In the early 19th century, "scientific" tricks were the rage because of public interest in new scientific discoveries. Some performers called themselves Doctor or Professor and gave a mock lecture before their act.

A French magician called Robert-Houdin (see next page) did a levitation illusion, claiming he used the newly-discovered gas, ether.

Great magic shows

At the end of the 19th and start of the 20th centuries spectacular magic shows travelled from theatre to theatre. One American illusionist, Howard Thurston, needed ten railway cars to transport all his equipment at one time.

Dante was born in Denmark. Sim Sala Bim were nonsense words from a Danish nursery rhyme.

Among the greatest of these showmen were Harry Blackstone Senior, Dante and his show called *Sim Sala Bim* and an Indian magician called P.C. Sorcar.

A home for magic

It was many magicians' dream to be able to stop travelling and perform in a permanent magic venue. Not many realized their dream.

One who did was John Nevil Maskelyne. With his partners, first George Cooke and later David Devant, he presented magic in the Egyptian Hall and later St. George's Hall in London for over 40 years from 1873.

Modern magic

In recent years, television has given magicians their largest audiences. The magic still thrills people, especially if they believe no camera tricks are used.

The future of magic

Advances in technology, such as holograms and lasers, may seem almost magical. Still, simple tricks done by a magician before your eyes are as baffling today as in ancient times. This is unlikely to change.

FAMOUS NAMES

Modern magic is usually said to have begun in the 19th century. Here are some of the most famous names in magic since that time.

Top hat and tails were common formal wear in the late 19th century.

The Father of modern magic

The French magician, Jean Eugène Robert-Houdin is often called the "Father of modern magic". He was an expert watchmaker and inventor who made gadgets for his home as well as magic props. He only took up magic full-time when he was over fifty. His original idea was to present himself as an ordinary man who just happened to be able to do extraordinary things.

The Wizard of the North

A Scotsman called John Henry Anderson was among the first to realize that success depended on good promotion. He made sure of large audiences by giving plenty of advance warning that he was coming to town and toured extensively in Britain and the United States in the 19th century. He sometimes billed himself by the catchy title The Wizard of the North.

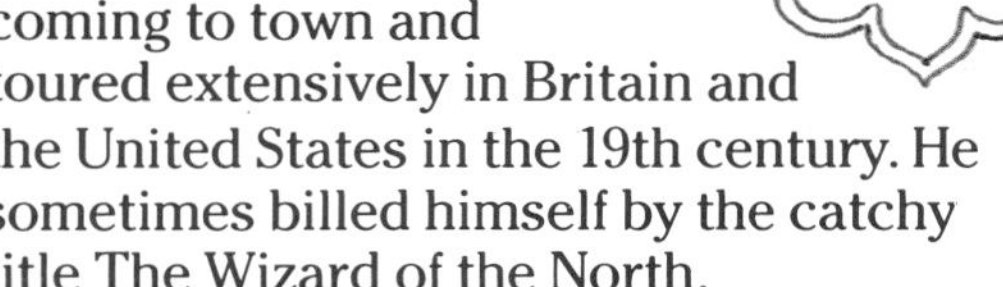

Individualists

As magic increased in popularity, entertainers had to do something different to get noticed.

◄ Chung Ling Soo was really William Ellsworth Robinson, an American imitating a Chinese magician. He kept up his Chinese persona at all times in public. He died on stage in 1918 attempting a trick in which he caught a bullet in his mouth. The gun was faulty and fired a real bullet that killed him.

Harry Houdini was ► born in 1874 in Hungary as Ehrich Weiss. He changed his name to Houdini as a tribute to Robert-Houdin. Possibly the greatest showman ever, his name became a household word through his daring feats of escapology.

Two American brothers, Ira and William Davenport, exploited the rage for spiritualism (contacting the dead) in the 19th century. They were tied up and locked in a cabinet from which strange noises and objects then emerged. They claimed these were supernatural. Really they were escape artists who did the effects themselves.

▼

Inventors

Some magicians are famous more for inventing a very famous trick than for their own performances.

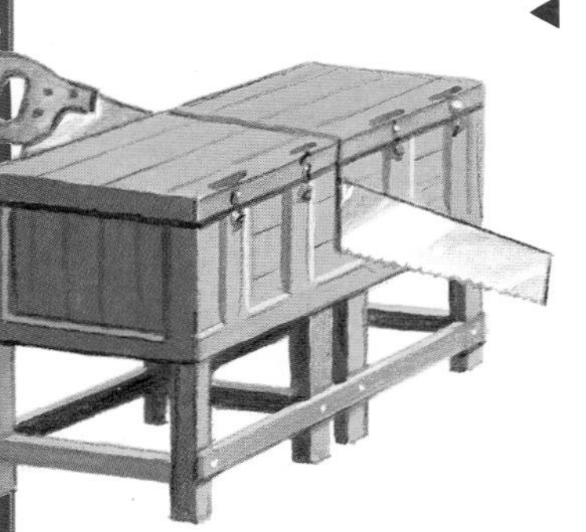

◀ In 1921, the British magician P.T. Selbit invented and performed for the first time the world's most famous trick, "Sawing Through a Woman".

Buatier de Kolta ▶ invented the "Vanishing Birdcage" in which a live canary disappeared with its cage. It caused an uproar over cruelty to the canary. In Britain a magician even did the trick for politicians to satisfy them that no harm came to the bird. Some say the trick was done differently in the test and the canary was lucky this time.

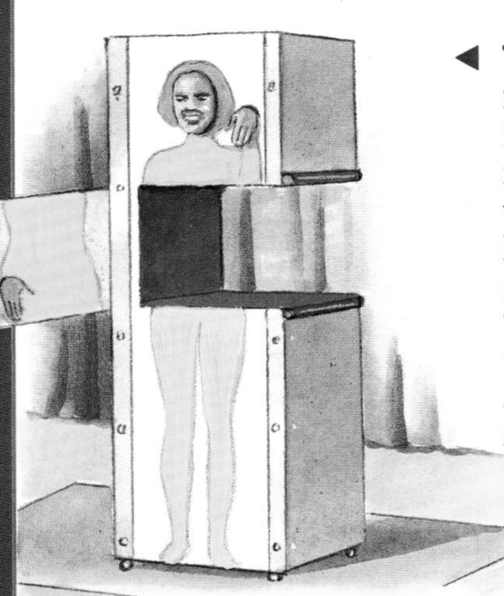

◀ The most famous inventor of recent times was Robert Harbin. He invented the "Zig-Zag Girl" trick, in which a girl's middle seems to be removed.

Kings of manipulation

T. Nelson Downs was called the ▶ King of Koins because of his spectacular silent act with coins.

◀ Cardini seemed to produce dozens of fans of cards from nowhere. He learned his skills in World War I trenches, where it was so cold that he practiced in gloves. Later, white gloves and a monocle became his trademarks.

Channing Pollock was the most ▶ famous producer of live doves. His style and act have been copied many times.

Close-up

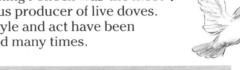

Not many close-up artists become widely known as they can only perform for a few people at once. Perhaps the most famous in this century were Max Malini and Nate Leipzig. Another great close-up performer, Canadian-born Dai Vernon, has recorded their lives and tricks.

Magicians on television

Television has made many magicians famous, including Fred Kaps from Holland, Britain's Paul Daniels and David Copperfield from the United States.

In the 1970s, a man called Uri Geller frequently entertained on television. He claimed to bend forks and make watches stop or start by the power of his mind. Magicians say they can duplicate all his effects.

CARDS: FIRST HANDLING SKILLS

Playing cards can be used in a wider variety of tricks than any other prop. On the next six pages you can learn to handle them expertly. The actual cards may vary but these skills apply to any pack.

When you try any trick in this part of the book, first read the steps and look at the pictures carefully. Remember that how to do it is only one side of the trick. You must think of good presentations, too.

About playing cards

Cards are cheap, colorful and easy to obtain, so they are ideal to start doing magic with.

Decks of cards come in different sizes. Use whichever suits you best.

The deck, or a card, is "face-down" when you can see the patterned back and "face-up" when you can see the value and suit.

Look for decks with a white border around the pattern on the back. This helps disguise various secret moves as it is the same color as the face of the card.

It is well worth mastering basic handling skills before trying to perform any tricks.

Overhand Shuffle

This simple but effective shuffle can be adapted to help in tricks (see the Shuffle Control on page 35).

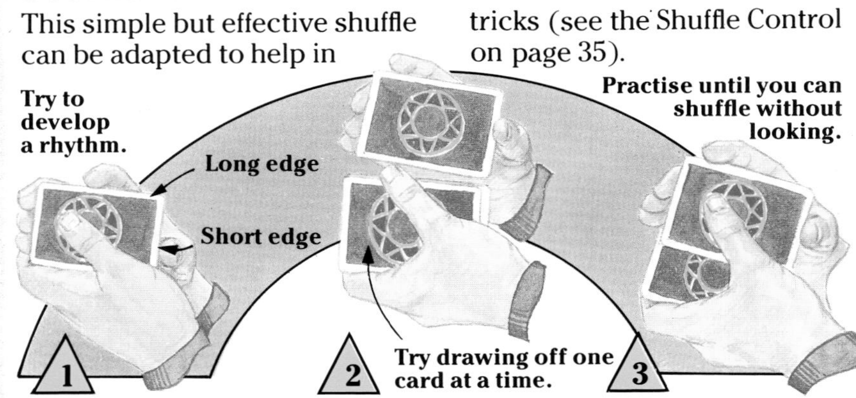

Try to develop a rhythm.
Long edge
Short edge
Practise until you can shuffle without looking.
Try drawing off one card at a time.
1
2
3

1. Rest the deck on a long edge in your left hand. Hold the short edges with your right fingers and thumb.
2. Press on the deck with your left thumb. Lift your right hand and draw some cards into your left.
3. Lift the deck over the drawn-off cards and repeat 2 and 3 until all the cards are in your left hand.

Squaring the deck

After shuffling, you may need to tidy, or square, the deck. Tap the edges on a table to make them even or use your hands like this:

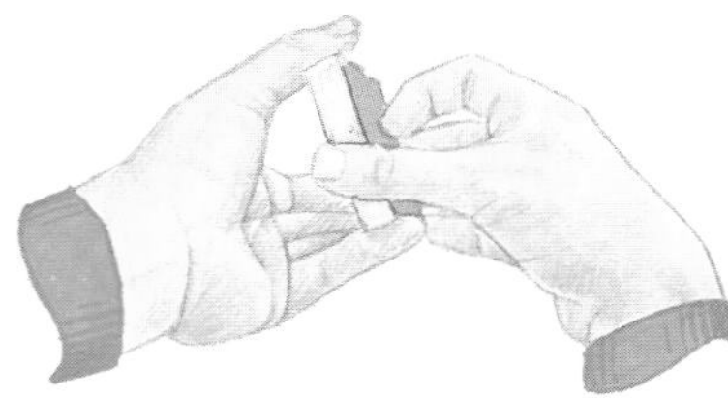

The Three Burglars

This is a self-working trick, which means that it doesn't need any slight of hand, but you should still work on the presentation. To prepare, put a red ace on top of the face-down deck and a three on the bottom. You can do this by looking through the cards, face-up, and cutting them into place. Chat while you do it, then put the cards down for a moment before going on so people forget what you were up to.

1. Openly search the deck and take out the other threes and red ace. Put them on a table, face-down, with the ace on the bottom. Place the deck by them.

Point out that the ace is red, but not its suit.

2. Tell the audience that the deck is a house and the threes are burglars. Show them a three then put it on top of the deck, saying this burglar got in by the roof.

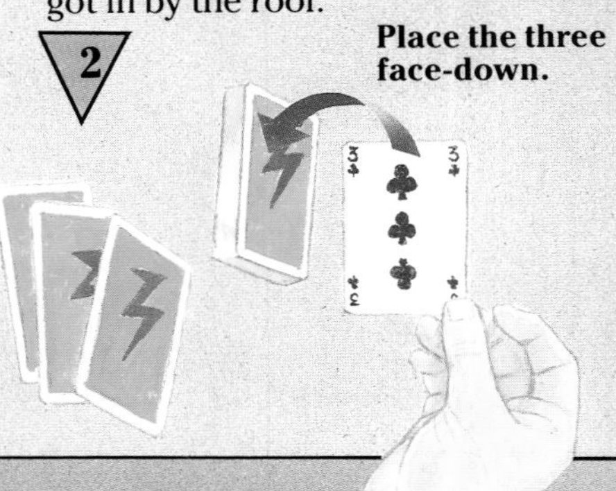

Place the three face-down.

Cutting the cards

Cutting means dividing the deck in two and putting the half that was on the bottom on the top. However many times you cut the deck, the order of the cards does not change. You can cut the cards on a table. The Kick Cut, below, is a neat way to do it in your hands.

Kick Cut

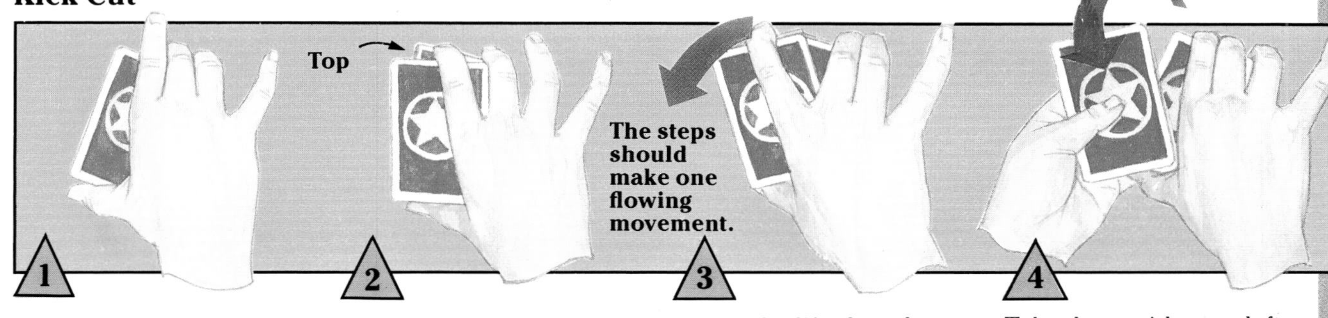

Top
The steps should make one flowing movement.
1
2
3
4

1. Hold the deck face-down by its short edges with your right fingers and thumb.
2. With your right first finger, lift about half the cards off the deck at the top short edge.
3. Swivel the lifted cards to the left, pivoting on your thumb, ready to take in your left hand.
4. Take them with your left hand, then put the cards that are in your right hand on top.

Classic Card Spread

Many card tricks involve a spectator picking a card. The magician often spreads the cards to let him choose. This is how to do a Classic Spread. Do it in a straight line or make a slight fan-shape. Note that the cards are in the same order when you close them together again.

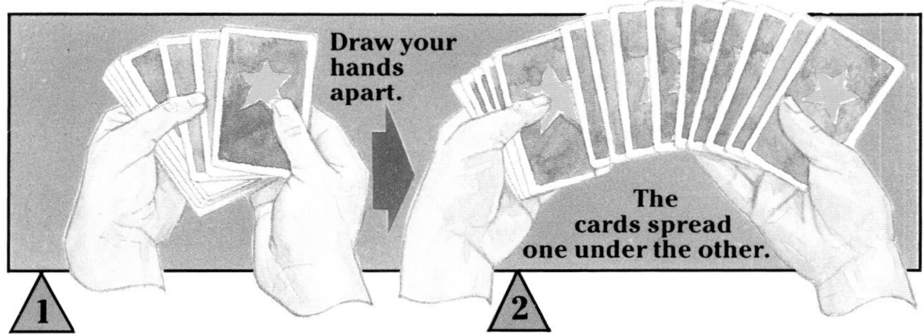

Draw your hands apart.
The cards spread one under the other.
1
2

1. Hold the deck flat in your left hand. With your left thumb, push cards off the top of the deck into your right hand a few at a time.
2. Spread the cards into a rough line or fan. Support them with your fingers underneath and your thumbs on top.

Say the next burglar got in by the cellar (put a three under the deck). The third climbed in a top floor window (put this card in a third down the deck).

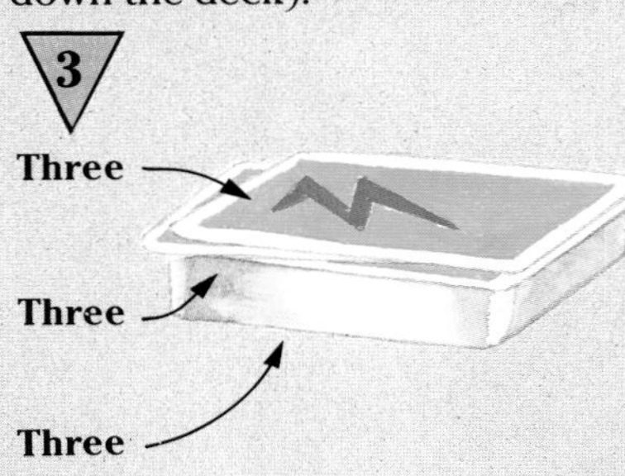

Pick up the ace and say it is a policeman who enters the ground floor (put it in two thirds down the deck). Cut the pack a few times, saying there is a chase.

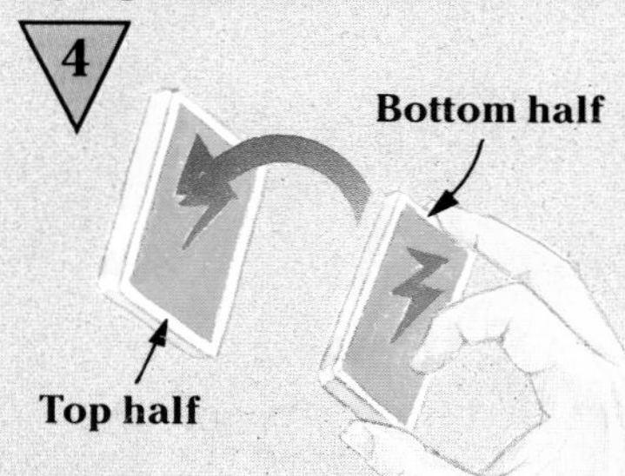

Spread the cards face-up. A red ace and three threes will appear together somewhere in the deck so you can say that the policeman caught the burglars.

This is the ace from the top of the deck, not the "policeman". No-one should notice as they are both red.

The Glimpse

It is often useful to know the bottom card of the deck. To Glimpse it, ask a spectator to shuffle; if the deck is handed back face-up, you will see the bottom card. If not, square the deck on the table and glance at it then.

Only turn the cards slightly towards you.

Card Spread and Flourish

How to spread cards in your hands is shown on page 31. The top two pictures here show a spread to do on a table. Read how to do it on the right. Practice until you can do it evenly. Then add the flourish in the bottom picture.

Do As I Do

You use two decks of cards, and the Glimpse and Spread techniques above in this trick. Place the decks on a table and ask a volunteer to take one and copy you exactly. Pick up your pack and start shuffling. Then follow these steps, shown from the magician's point of view.

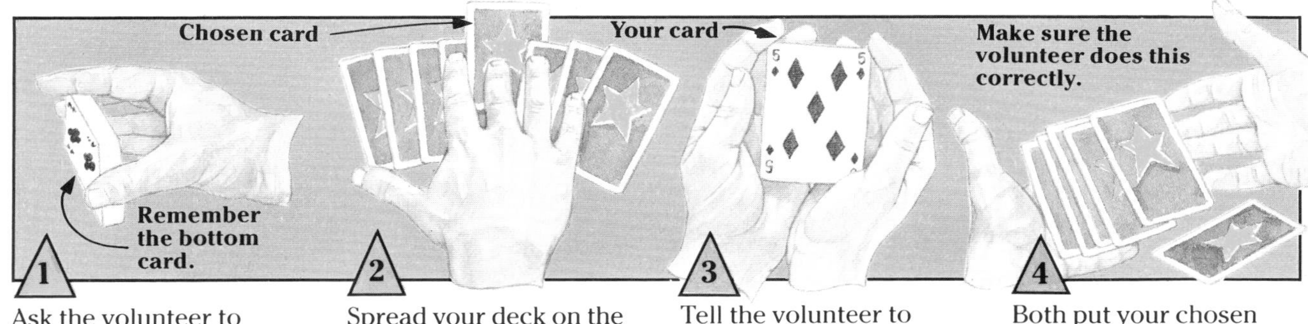

1. Ask the volunteer to swap decks with you. Before handing him your deck, square it and do the Glimpse.

2. Spread your deck on the table. Swing your finger as if choosing, then bring it down on a card. The volunteer does it, too.

3. Tell the volunteer to memorize his chosen card. Only pretend to memorize yours (you do not need to know it).

4. Both put your chosen cards aside, face-down. Gather up the decks, keeping the cards in the same order.

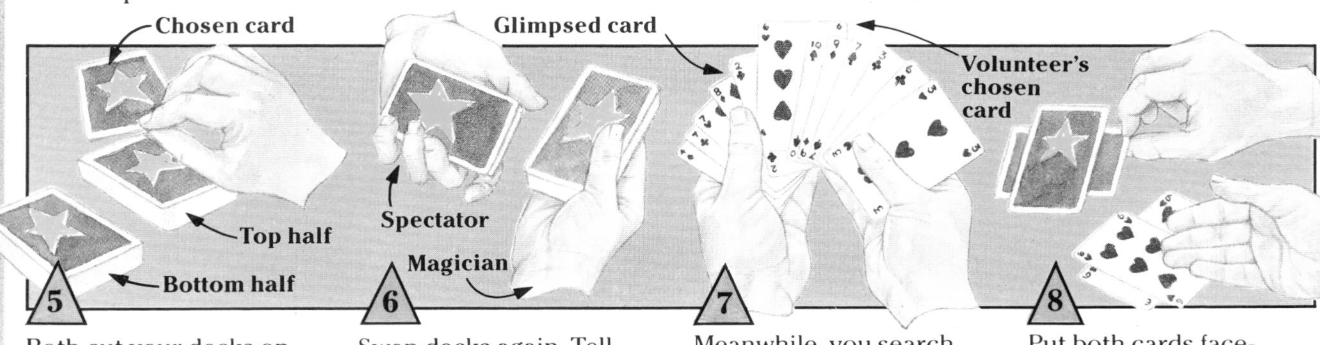

5. Both cut your decks on the table. Put your chosen card on the top half before completing the cut. Now cut again.

6. Swap decks again. Tell the volunteer to search the pack, find the card he memorized and take it out.

7. Meanwhile, you search for the Glimpsed card and take the one on top of it. Try to finish before the volunteer.

8. Put both cards face-down on the table, one crossways on top of the other. Turn both over. They are the same.

The cards make an overlapping line.

The Spread

◀ Touch the short edges of the deck with your right fingers and thumb. Tap the left side of the cards with your first finger and sweep them to the right.

The Flourish

◀ With your left hand, flip the card on the left face-up. A chain reaction turns all the cards over with a ripple.

Key Card Control

A Control is a way of getting a card to where you want it in the deck. In this Control, you use a Key Card to find an unknown card and bring it to the top. You can use it in many tricks.

1. Glimpse the bottom card. It is the Key Card.

2. Spread the deck and have a card chosen.

3. Cut the deck in two, have the chosen card placed on the top half, then complete the cut.

4. Get the spectator to cut the deck a few times. The Key Card stays with the chosen one.

5. Spread the deck face-up and say something like, "Your card is lost somewhere in here, would you agree?" as an excuse for looking.

6. Spot the Key Card. The chosen card is on top of it.

7. Take the chosen card and those above it in one hand and the Key Card and those below it in the other. Cut the half with the chosen card to the top. Keep talking to misdirect.

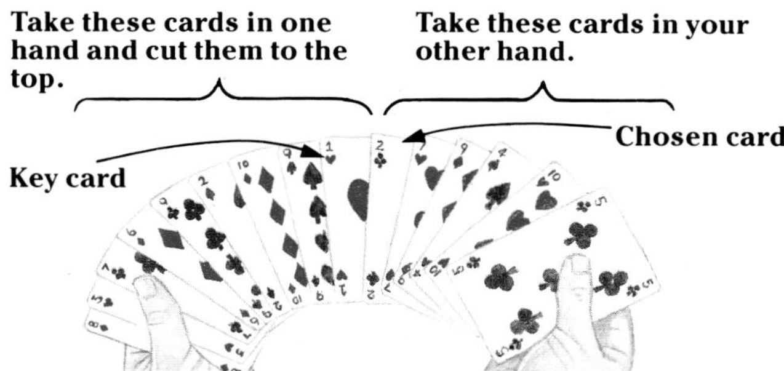
Take these cards in one hand and cut them to the top.
Take these cards in your other hand.
Chosen card
Key card

Turn-Around Card

Start with steps 1 to 4 of the Key Card Control (see left) so that the chosen card is next to the Key Card. Now ask the spectator to watch.

Start to deal the cards (take them off the deck one at a time) onto the table, turning them face-up. When you see the Key Card, remember the card that follows it (the chosen card). Deal a few more cards.

Now take a card as if to deal it but don't turn it over. Say that the next card you turn over will be the chosen one. Ask the spectator if he believes you. He should say no, as he has already seen his card dealt.

The spectator assumes you will turn over the card in your hand, so should insist you are wrong. Argue a bit, then replace the held card on the pack, look among the dealt cards, find the chosen one and turn it face-down.

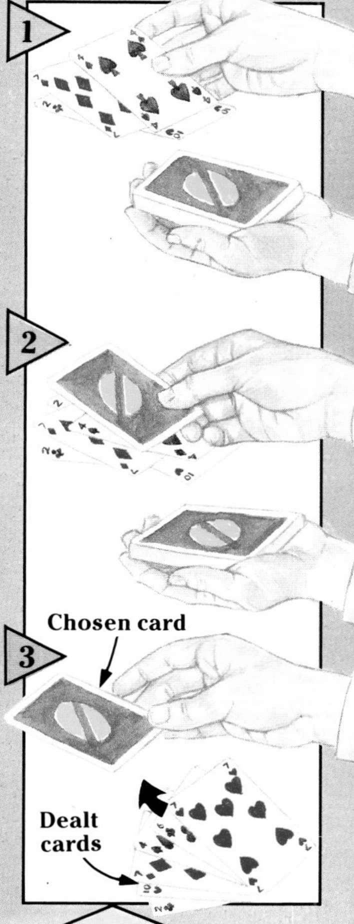
1
2
3
Chosen card
Dealt cards

Sucker tricks

A trick like Turn-Around Card is called a "sucker" trick because it makes the spectator look silly. He is convinced that you will be proved wrong, but you turn the tables. Don't use too many sucker tricks or appear too pleased when you do, or the audience may be offended. It is only a joke, so treat it lightly.

Forces

A Force is a way of making sure that a spectator chooses a particular card. Two kinds of Force are shown below. There are lots of others. If you genuinely allow the spectator a totally free choice of card it is called a "fair selection".

Cut Force

Have the card you want chosen on top of the deck. Ask a spectator to cut the deck in two on the table. Put the bottom half crossways on the top half.

It is important misdirection to let some time pass so everyone forgets what has happened.

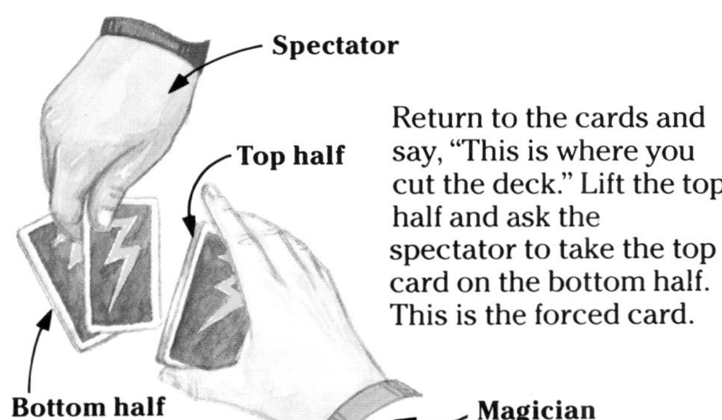

Return to the cards and say, "This is where you cut the deck." Lift the top half and ask the spectator to take the top card on the bottom half. This is the forced card.

Classic Force

This is considered the best force but it is quite hard and requires some nerve. The best way to practice is to try it out even when a fair selection would do for a trick.

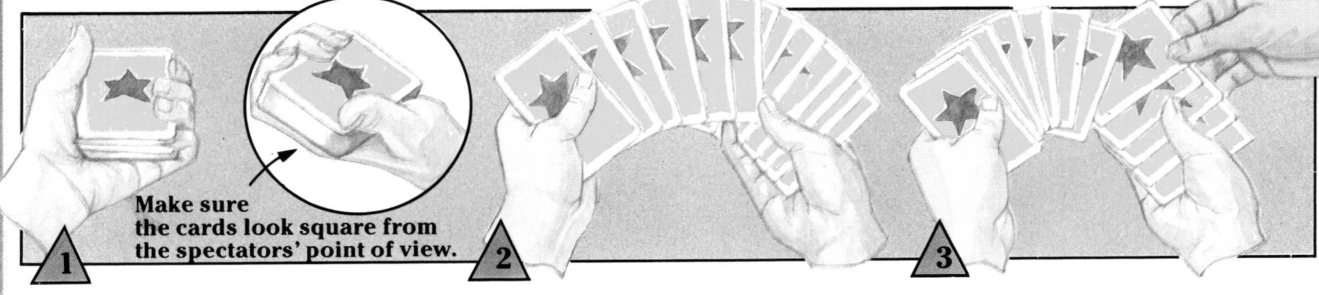

the cards look square from

1. Glimpse the bottom card. Kick-Cut the deck. As you complete the cut, curl your little finger over the top half. Then put the bottom half on top of it.

2. Spread the cards for a spectator to choose. Your little finger stays trapped in place to keep track of the Glimpsed card.

3. Time the spread so that the Glimpsed card is right under the spectator's fingers as she chooses a card. You will be surprised at how often it works.

Double Lift

Use the Double Lift when you want to seem to show the top card of a deck.

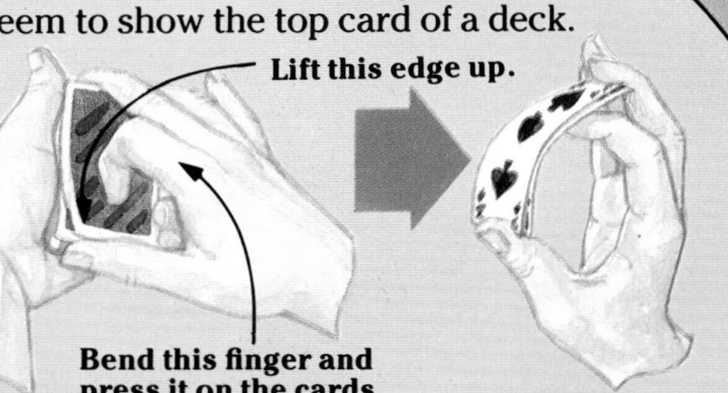

Lift this edge up.
Bend this finger and
press it on the cards.

Take the deck in your left hand. Hold the short edges with your right fingers and thumb. With your right thumb, bend up the top two cards and lift them off as one.

Instant Revelation

1. Have a card selected. Then have it returned to the deck and control it to the top by the Shuffle Control.

2. Pick up the deck and show the bottom card to the spectator. Ask casually if this is her card. She should say no.

Shuffle Control

This is another way to get a chosen card to the top of the deck.

1 Start an Overhand Shuffle. About half way through, stop and ask the volunteer to place her card on top of the cards that have already been shuffled.

2 Carry on by shuffling off a single card and letting it fall out of line with the rest of the deck. It should stick out towards you a tiny bit. This is called "in-jogging".

3 Don't pause, but shuffle the rest of the cards normally. Spectators will not notice the in-jogged card. Take the cards below the in-jogged one and cut them to the top. The chosen card is now on the top.

3 Do the Double Lift and show the spectator what appears to be the top card. Ask if this is her card. She will say no. Replace the card(s).

4 Hand the deck to the spectator and ask her to tap lightly on the top card. Then tell her to turn it over and she reveals her card.

Countdown

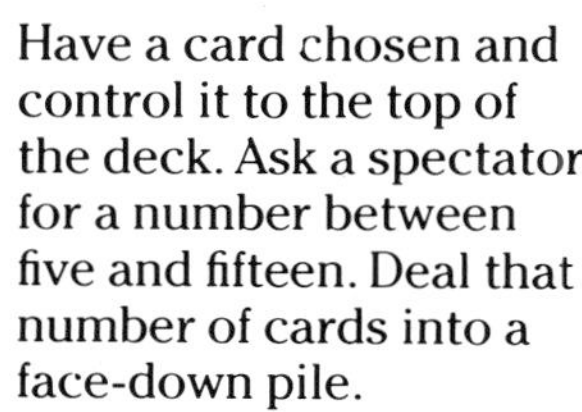

1 Have a card chosen and control it to the top of the deck. Ask a spectator for a number between five and fifteen. Deal that number of cards into a face-down pile.

2 Count the cards out loud as you deal. When you say the last number, turn that card face-up, claiming this is the chosen card. It isn't, so pretend to be puzzled or embarrassed.

3 Suddenly "realize" that you forgot the magic words, or some similar excuse. Turn the face-up card back over again, pick up all the cards you dealt and put them on top of the deck.

Dealt cards

4 Say some magic words or do something else suitable to correct what was supposed to be your "mistake" in the previous step.

Do a "magic tap".

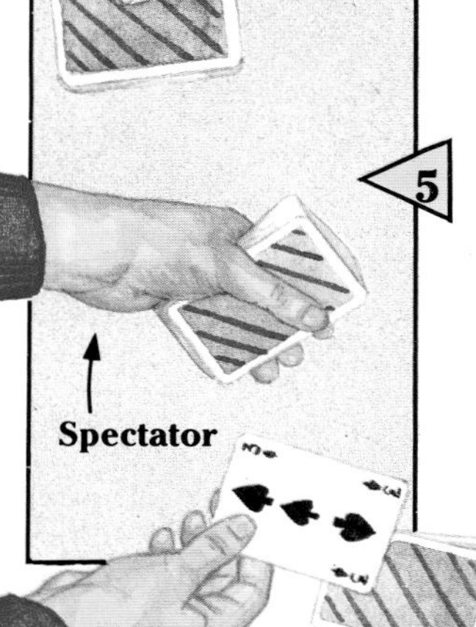

5 Ask the spectator to do the countdown again, just as you did it. This time, when the last card is turned over, it is the correct one. This way the magic "happens" in the spectator's hands, not yours.

CLOSE-UP COINS

If you did the French Drop on page 8 you already know one coin slight. Here are some more you should master if you want to do coin tricks. Practice the Palms (palming means to hide in your hand) and Coin Switch before trying the tricks.

Finger Palm

Bend your two middle fingers and hold the coin in them. Let the others curl naturally.

Thumb Palm

Hold the coin flat between your first and second fingers.

Curl your fingers and pinch the edge of the coin flat between your thumb and palm.

Relax your fingers. You cannot move your thumb, but try not to let it look awkward.

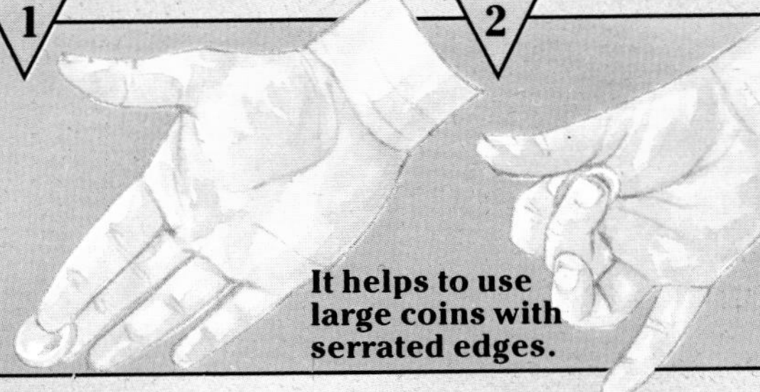

1
2
3
It helps to use large coins with serrated edges.
Reverse the steps to retrieve the coin.

Classic Palm

Press the coin onto your palm with your two middle fingers. Squeeze the fleshy base of your thumb over it to hold it. Straighten your fingers. This is the best Palm, but the hardest to do.

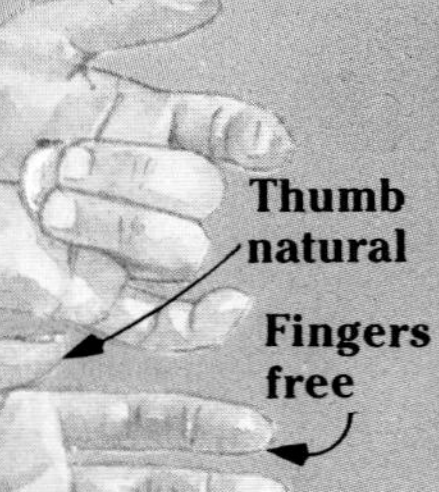

Thumb Palm Vanish

Hold the coin as in step 1, above. Slightly cup your left hand as if you are going to take the coin in it.

Put your right fingers into your left hand. Thumb Palm the coin in your right hand while hidden by your left.

Move your left hand away as if it has the coin. Relax your right. Now when you open your left hand it is empty.

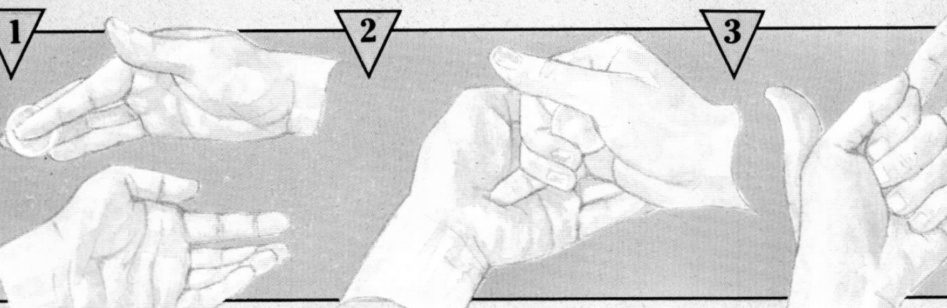

Quick trick

Do a French Drop or Thumb Palm Vanish into your right hand. Show that the coin has gone. Now squeeze your nose with your right hand and let the coin drop into your left.

Copper and Silver

In this trick you make a copper and a silver coin swap places. Take the two coins from a pocket with your right hand. In the same hand, Finger Palm a second copper coin.

Hold up one copper and one silver coin in your fingers. Place the silver one to your left and the copper one to your right on a table in front of you.

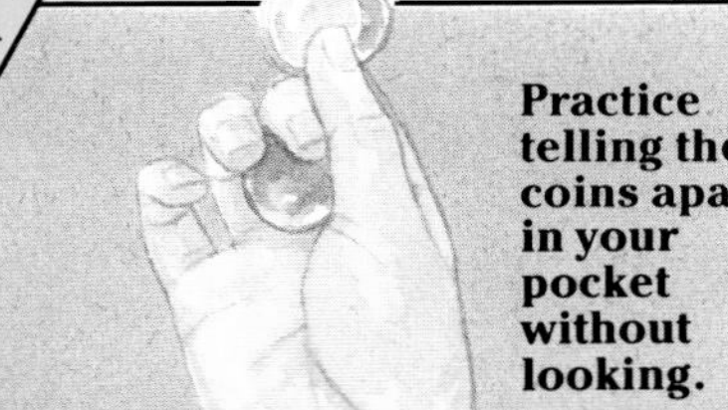

1
2
Practice telling the coins apart in your pocket without looking.

Top Pocket Vanish

This is a good trick to confuse people who always think a coin that has vanished must be in the other hand. You need to wear a shirt with a pocket. Do the Thumb Palm Vanish on the page opposite, but don't open your left hand. Then follow these steps.

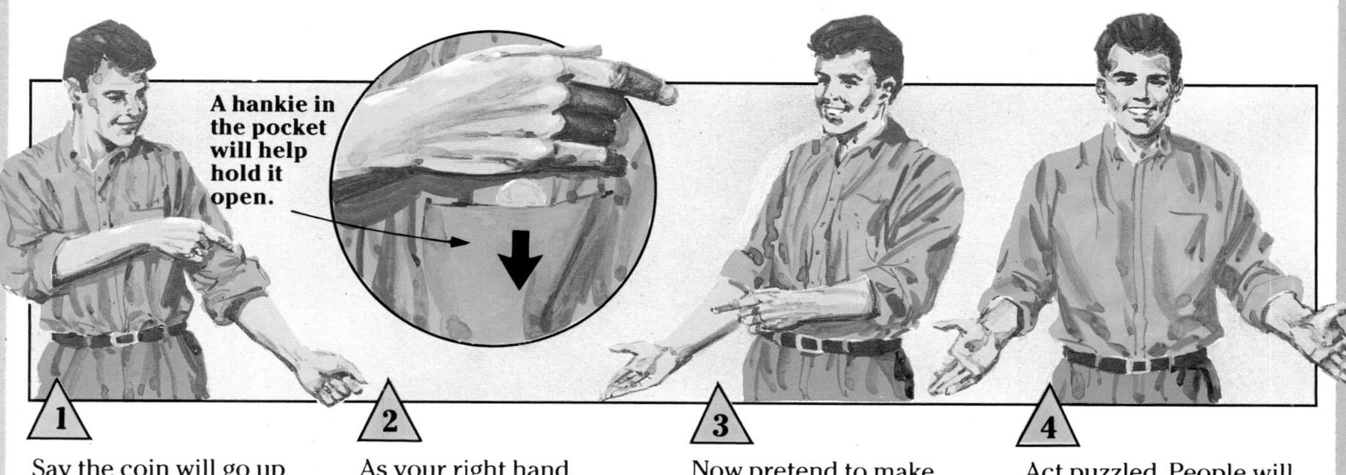

A hankie in the pocket will help hold it open.

1 Say the coin will go up your left arm, across your chest, down your right arm to your right hand. Trace this path with your right finger.

2 As your right hand passes your top pocket, drop the coin into it. Try to do it smoothly and without hesitating in your explanation.

3 Now pretend to make the coin move as described. Follow its supposed path with your eyes. Open your right hand. The coin is not there.

4 Act puzzled. People will assume the coin is still in your left hand. Open that hand, too, to show that the coin has vanished.

Coin Switch

In one hand, Finger Palm a copper coin and hold a silver coin between the first finger and thumb.

1 **Silver coin thrown into right hand.**

2 Toss the silver coin into the other hand and close your fingers round it at once. Do it several times.

3 **Silver coin drops into Finger Palm.**

Then make the same motion, but actually toss the copper coin and palm the silver one. Try the Switch from both hands.

Copper coin thrown into right hand.

3 Pick up the silver coin with your right fingers. Say you will hold it in your left hand. Do the Coin Switch from your right to your left hand.

4 Pick up the copper coin on the table with your right fingertips. Tell the spectators to watch carefully.

5 Make a magic gesture. Then let the two coins slide onto the table from the opposite hands to what is expected, as shown in the next step.

6 Let the copper coin slide from your left hand. Simultaneously Thumb Palm the copper coin in your right and release the silver one.

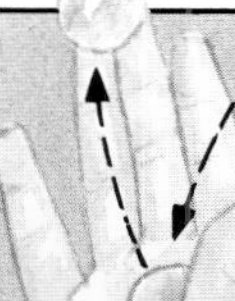

CLOSE-UP WITH OTHER PROPS

You can do tricks with lots of everyday things, such as dice, a glass or sugar lumps. Each one may not be as versatile as coins or cards, but doing magic with them is effective if you just pick them off a table or borrow them from somebody.

The Paddle Move

The Paddle Move is often done with two small paddle-shaped sticks with spots on. Here you can see how to do it with dice.

1 Take a dice in your first finger and thumb. Have the 6 facing you and the 3 on the face to the left of the 6 as you look at it.

4

2 Turn your hand to show the face of the dice opposite the 6. Now, the 1 faces you. Reverse the move by turning your hand back again.

These two moves should look identical. If you alternate them, the number on the face opposite the 6 seems to change each time.

3 Turn your hand again, but this time turn the dice round by one face, too, so the 2 is towards you. This is the Paddle Move.

Turn the dice in the same direction as your hand.

Reverse the Paddle Move by turning the dice back round by one face the other way as you turn your hand back.

Dice Swap

1 Hold two dice like this: left dice has 6 facing you and 3 under your first finger; right dice has 3 facing you and 6 under your finger.

2 Show the audience the 6 and 3 that are facing you. Turn your hand over normally to show 1 and 4 on the opposite sides.

3 Turn your hand back to its original position, doing the Paddle Move. The audience sees 6 and 3 again (on different dice, but don't point this out).

4 Reverse the Paddle Move to show the 1 and 4 again. Now point out that the 1 is on the left dice. Reverse the Paddle Move to show the 6 and 3 again.

5 Ask people which dice now has 1 on the other side. They should say the left dice. Turn your hand not doing the Paddle Move to reveal the 1 on the right dice.

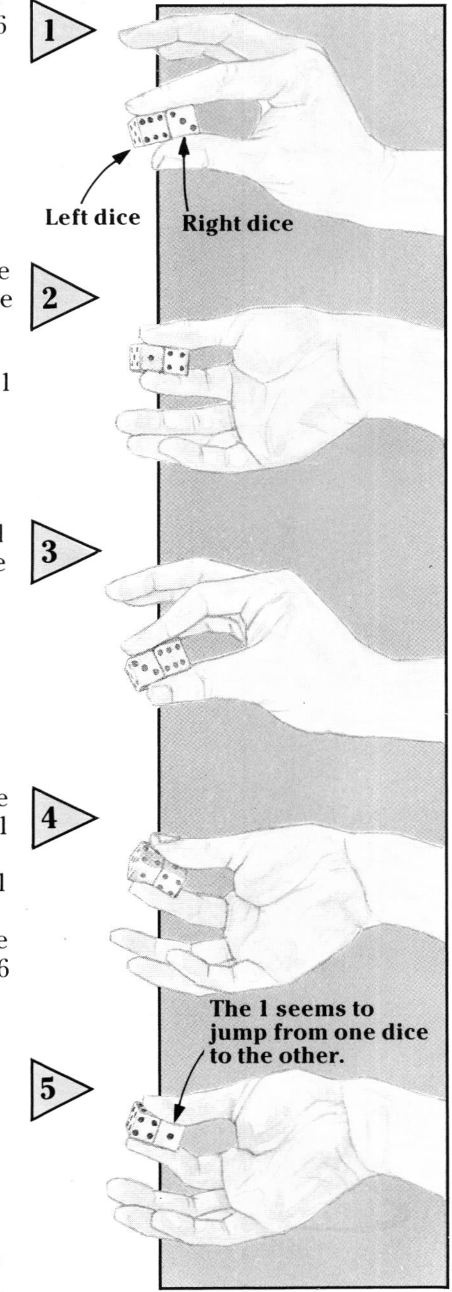

Left dice
Right dice
The 1 seems to jump from one dice to the other.

Sugar Lump Jump

This trick looks good if you can pick some sugar lumps from a bowl on the table. To make it easier to follow, the directions are written in a kind of code. Here is the key to it:

Key SL=sugar lump
LH=left hand
RH=right hand

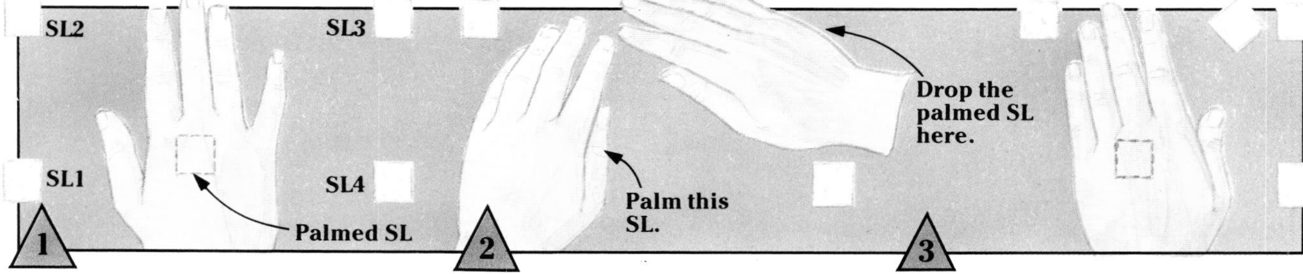

1. Classic Palm (see page 36) one SL in your RH. Place four more SL on a table as shown above. Number them in your head.

2. Cover SL1 with your LH and SL3 with your RH. Release the palmed SL and Classic Palm SL1 in your left hand.

3. Lift your hands to reveal two SL at position 3 and none at 1. You now have a SL palmed in your left hand. Carry on as below.

In each step, drop the palmed SL and palm the other:

4. LH over SL3; RH over SL4.
5. RH over SL3; LH over SL2.

6. Take all the SL in LH (with palmed SL) and replace in bowl.

Glass Through Table

For this trick you need to be sitting at a table. You use a small tumbler glass (without a stem) and a paper napkin. These things may be on the table, if it is set for a meal.

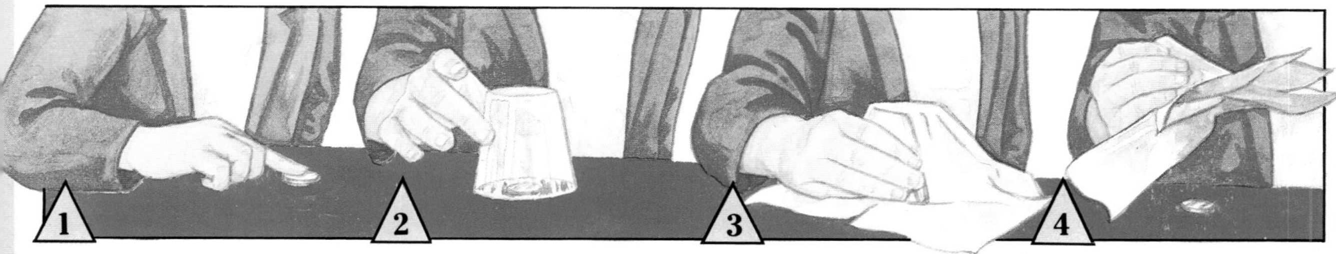

1. Borrow a coin and place it near the edge of the table. Claim you are going to make it pass through the table.

2. Say you must hide the coin and turn the glass over on top of it. As it is see-through, say you must cover it up.

3. Take a paper napkin and drape it over the glass. Mould it firmly round the shape of the glass.

4. Say some magic words and lift the napkin and glass up. The coin is still there. Act upset and replace the glass.

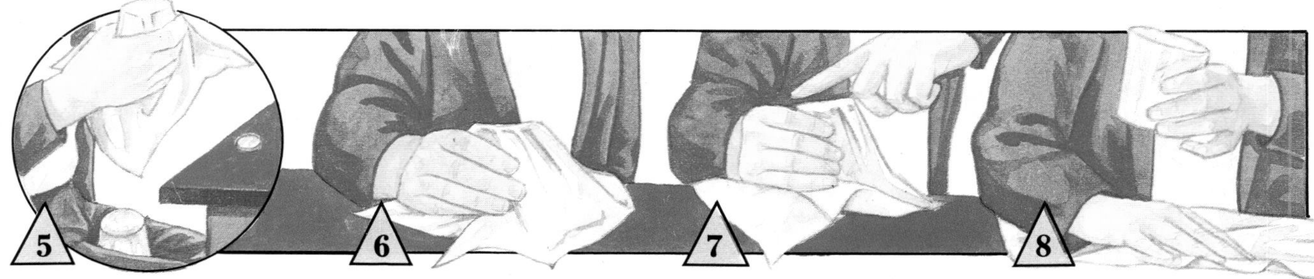

5. Repeat step 4, lifting napkin and glass over the edge of the table. Drop the glass unseen into your lap.

6. Hold the napkin gently to keep the glass shape. The coin is still there. Say you will try again. Put the napkin over it.

7. Say that as the coin will not perform properly, you will make the glass do it instead (people think it is still there).

8. Flatten the napkin with one hand and bring the glass out from under the table with the other.

SILENT MAGIC: CARD MANIPULATION

Many magicians who work silently use manipulation. This is the art of handling small props with great dexterity and performing tricks purely by slight of hand. On the next six pages you can learn basic manipulation skills with cards, coins, billiard balls and thimbles. They are quite hard and take a long time to perfect, but don't be put off. Practicing and improving is enjoyable in itself.

The Thumb Fan

1. Hold the deck of cards in your left hand, clasped between your thumb and palm.

2. Put your right thumb against the top left edge and push the cards to the right. Push the cards on the bottom of the pile first.

3. Run your right thumb across the tops of the cards in a curve to make a fan. The cards swivel under your left thumb.

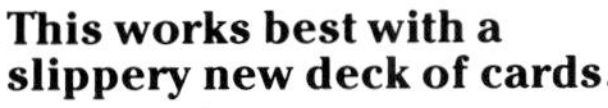

This works best with a slippery new deck of cards.

The Back Palm

This card palm is basic to card manipulation. Follow the steps below to vanish and re-produce a card. You must blend the individual steps into a smooth, rapid action.

The vanish

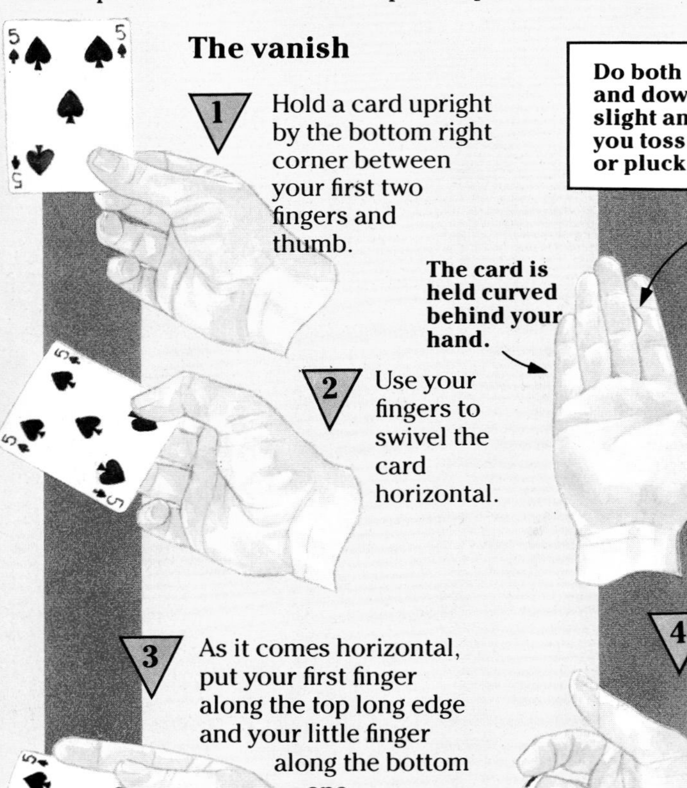

1. Hold a card upright by the bottom right corner between your first two fingers and thumb.

2. Use your fingers to swivel the card horizontal.

3. As it comes horizontal, put your first finger along the top long edge and your little finger along the bottom one.

4. Curl your second and third fingers towards your palm and push them against the short edge of the card to flip it over.

5. Let go with your thumb, straighten your fingers and clip the corners of the card between your first and second and third and fourth fingers. It disappears behind your hand.

The card is held curved behind your hand.

Work on stopping the corners poking out.

Do both moves with a swift up and down gesture. It hides the slight and looks as though you toss the card into thin air or pluck it from nowhere.

The re-production

6. To re-produce the card, keep your first finger straight but bend the others so that you can grab the corner of the card with your thumb.

Springing the Deck

This is an impressive flourish but is quite difficult. Practice over your bed or into a box to stop the cards flying everywhere.

1 Hold the deck by its short edges. Bend it in towards your palm. Put your other hand beneath

2 Release cards one by one and catch them. As you get better at it, move your hands apart.

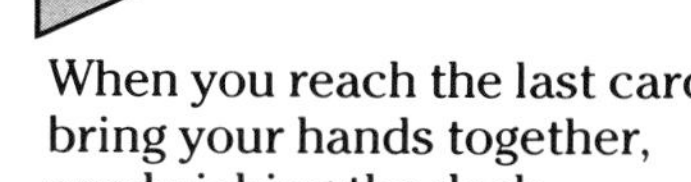

3 When you reach the last card, bring your hands together, sandwiching the deck.

Back Palming several cards

Once you can palm one card, put another in the same hand and follow steps 1-5 again. Slip the second card on top of the first. Build up until you can palm six or so at once.

Re-produce them by following steps 6-8, releasing only one card at a time. The hardest part is to keep hold of the palmed cards while you take or release another.

8 Continue to pull the card out with your thumb. Move your first finger out of the way so it can flip upright in front of your fingers.

7 Press down with your thumb and release the card from between your third and fourth fingers.

Basic Back Palm Routine

In this pose you can do the moves without revealing how.

1 Hold six cards in a small fan in your left hand. Stand with your left shoulder to the audience.

2 Take a card in your right hand. Pretend to toss it into the air, making it vanish using the Back Palm.

3 Repeat five times. You could look astonished as the cards vanish, or act as if it is perfectly normal.

4 After a pause, pretend to see something in the air, reach out and re-produce a card, as if from nowhere.

5 Take the re-produced card with your left hand. Or you could just let it drop onto the floor or a table.

6 Repeat until all six cards reappear. Make "seeing" the cards before you grab them as convincing as possible.

SILENT MAGIC: COIN MANIPULATION

Many coin tricks involve vanishing coins and re-producing them in an unusual way. The Miser's Dream, below, is probably the best-known one that can be performed silently on stage. To do it you need to learn the Edge Palm slight shown here.

The Edge Palm

This palm is sometimes called the Downs Palm after the American magician T. Nelson Downs, who invented it.

The coin is still flat.

View from on top.

View from the side.

1. Hold a coin flat between your first and second fingers.

2. Curl your fingers to put the coin in the crook of your thumb. Grip it between your thumb and first finger.

3. Keeping hold of the coin, straighten your fingers naturally. In the two pictures above you can see what it should look like to you from the side and from on top.

4. To re-produce the coin, Curl your fingers in and take it between your first and second fingers.

5. Straighten your fingers to reveal the coin held at the tips.

Make the coins disappear with a tossing motion. This helps hide the slight and makes it seem as if you throw the coins into thin air.

Talking coins

In coin tricks, if coins clink when they should not it is called "talking".

It may seem difficult to avoid talk at first, especially when handling more than one coin (see opposite), but keep trying and it will come.

The Miser's Dream

It is easiest to prepare this trick before coming on stage, so it is a good one to do first. In the trick, you seem to pluck coins from thin air to toss into a bucket. You can't Edge Palm enough coins for the whole trick, so after the first three you fool people with an illusion.

The bucket is shown transparent here so you can see.

Practice "seeing" a coin in empty air.

1. To prepare, Edge Palm 4 coins in your right hand. Hide 10 coins in your left hand, as shown above.

2. Pick up a bucket or tin with your left hand, as shown. Now you are ready. You seem just to be holding an empty bucket.

3. "See" a coin in mid-air. Reach for it, draw a coin from the Edge-Palm, display it and toss it in the bucket. Repeat twice.

Edge Palming lots of coins

Make sure people can't see the first coin as you pick the second up.

1 With one coin already held in the Edge Palm (see left), pick up another with your first finger and thumb.

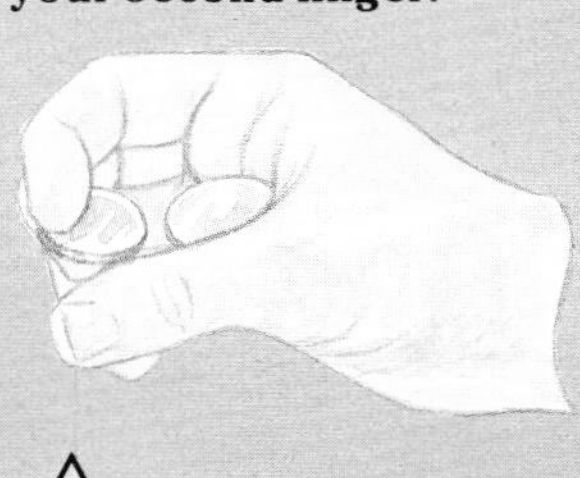

Support the coins with your second finger.

2 Put it between your first and second fingers. Then curl these fingers and slide the second coin under the first.

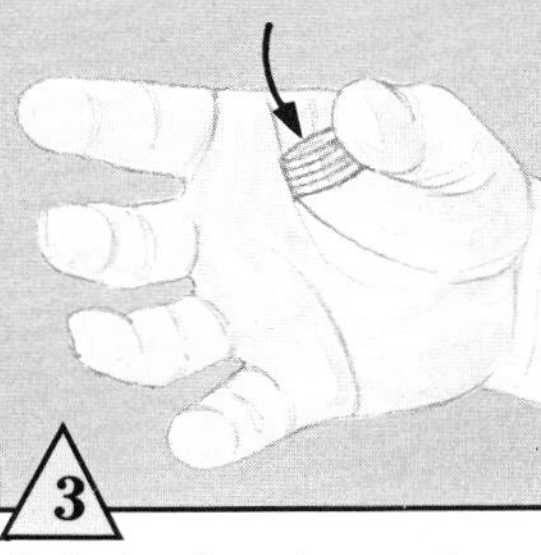

The coins must all be the same size.

3 Grip both coins and straighten your fingers as before. Repeat with as many coins as you are able to hold.

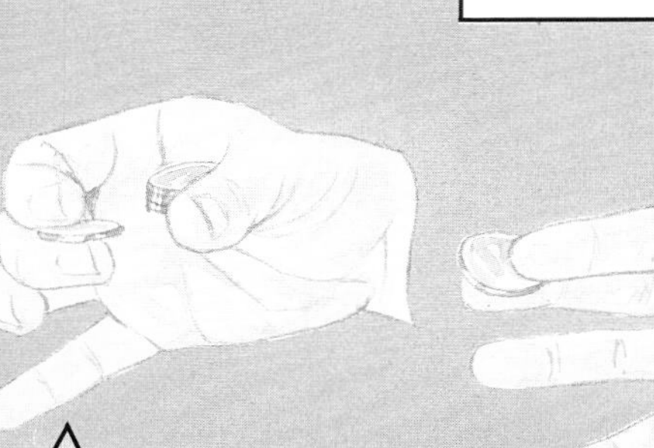

4 To re-produce coins one at a time, curl your second finger in under the stack of coins and slip the bottom one out.

5 When it has slid out far enough, clip it between your first and second fingers.

6 Straighten your fingers, with the coin held at the tips. Don't forget to keep gripping the coins that are still palmed.

Stealing and loads

Manipulators often need to get more props secretly while performing. This is called "stealing".

The prop you steal is called a "load". If it is attached to yourself, it is a "body-load". Loads can also be fixed to a table or chair. Always fix a body load to a part of your clothing that does not move. A jacket can swing, for instance, but trousers stay in the same place.

Pin the load somewhere hidden.

This picture shows a clip for holding cards to be stolen during an act. You can make one simply using a paper clip with a safety pin stuck through it.

The clink of the coin you drop makes people think you really threw another coin.

4 Take the last Edge Palmed coin and pretend to toss it in too, but really, re-palm it and drop a coin from your left hand.

5 Repeat step 4 nine times. You produce and Edge Palm the same coin each time and let a coin drop from your left hand with a clink. Be inventive about "finding" coins. You could pretend to make a spectator "catch" an invisible coin and throw it into the bucket.

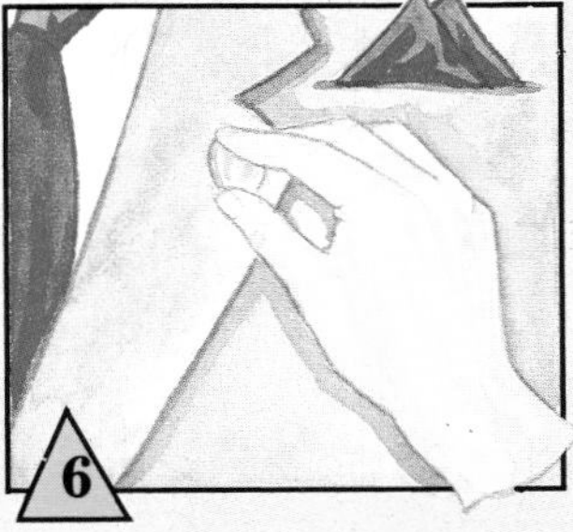

6 Or produce a coin from a spectator's lapel or behind his ear, for example. Ideas like these add variety.

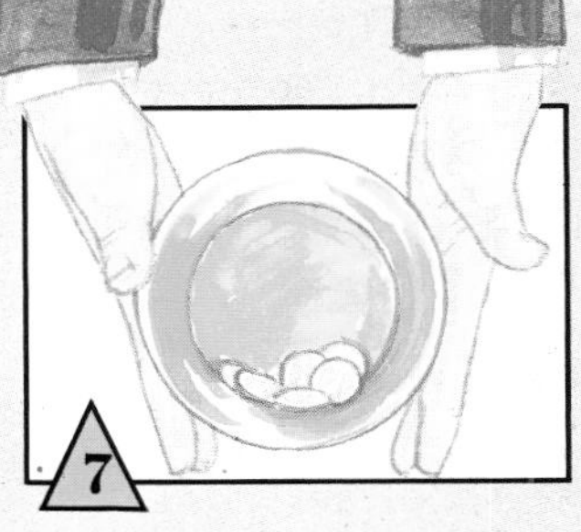

7 At the end, show all the coins in the bucket. This "proves" that you really threw them all in, in case people were suspicious.

MANIPULATING BILLIARD BALLS

Manipulating billiard balls is quite hard, especially if your hands are small. You can buy special balls in magic shops, which are lighter and easier to handle.

Ball Roll Flourish

1 Take a ball between your first and second fingers.

2 Bring your second finger forward, rolling the ball behind it. Put your third finger next to your first.

3 Now let go with your first finger and roll the ball round to between your second and third fingers.

4 Put your little finger behind, bring your third finger forward and roll the ball over it to between your third and little fingers.

5 From here, start to roll the ball back the other way by bringing your second finger in front as shown in step 6.

6 Roll the ball to between your third and second fingers. Bring your first finger forward and do the same again. Repeat from step 1.

Try to roll it faster and faster.

Billiard ball slights

These pictures show how slights you already know (pages 8 and 36) work with a billiard ball.

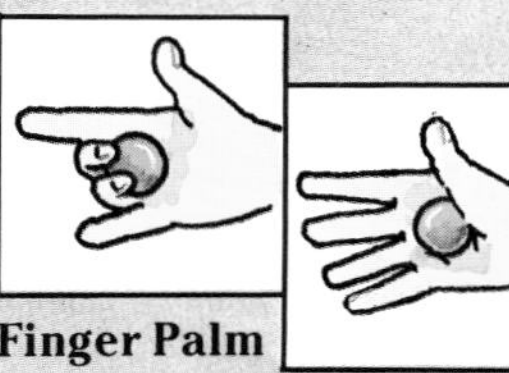

Finger Palm

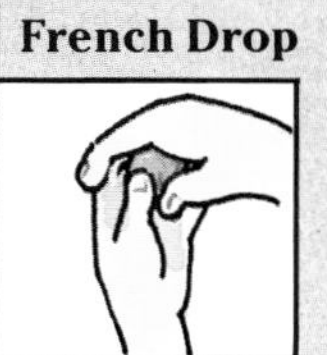

Classic Palm

French Drop

Swallowing the Ball

Do a French Drop to leave the ball in your right hand. Lift your left hand and pretend to eat the ball. Rub your stomach with your right hand and re-produce it.

Bottom of Fist Vanish

When you practice this slight, make the move for real first, (a rehearsal technique suggested on page 16), to feel how the ball's weight affects your movements.

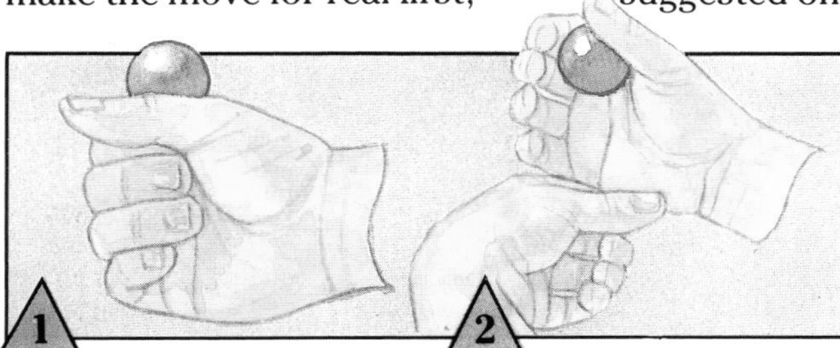

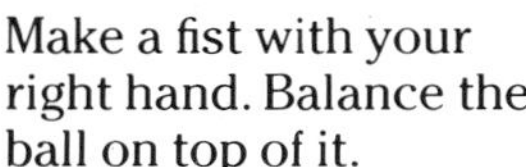

Ball palmed in right hand.

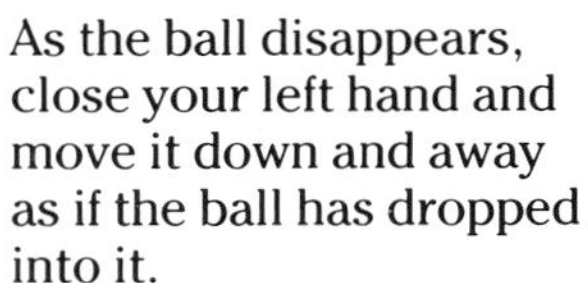

1 Make a fist with your right hand. Balance the ball on top of it.

2 Loosen your fingers to let the ball drop into your hand. Hold your left hand as if to catch it underneath.

3 As the ball disappears, close your left hand and move it down and away as if the ball has dropped into it.

4 Pretend to jiggle the ball in your left hand, then open your hand to show the ball has gone.

MANIPULATING THIMBLES

Thimbles are also frequently used by manipulators. Because they are small and light, they are easier to practise with than billiard balls. See how to make a thimble holder on page 58.

Thumb Palm

Practice putting the thimble in the Thumb Palm from your second and third fingers, too.

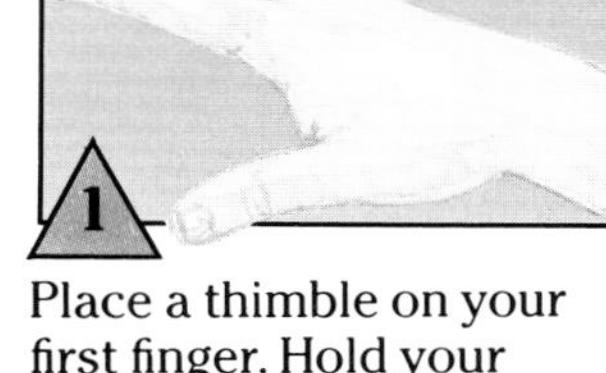

1 Place a thimble on your first finger. Hold your hand outstretched.

2 Curl your first finger into the crook of your thumb and take the thimble between your thumb and palm.

3 Straighten your finger, leaving the thimble held by your thumb. It is completely hidden.

Thumb Palm Vanish

Try to make the steps look like one continuous movement.

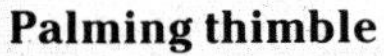

Palming thimble

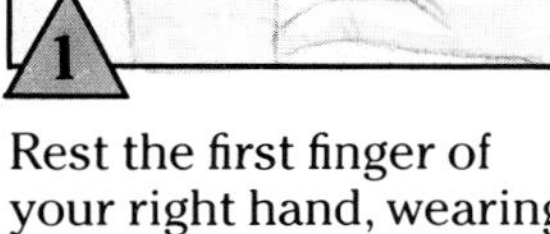

1 Rest the first finger of your right hand, wearing the thimble, on the open palm of your left hand.

2 Turn your left hand over to hide the thimble. Quickly thumb palm it and straighten your finger again.

3 Curl your left hand round your finger and slide it up and off as if pulling the thimble from your fingertip.

4 A moment or two later, you can open your left hand to show that the thimble has vanished.

Jumping Thimbles

This trick uses two identical thimbles and the Thumb Palm to make it look as if a thimble is jumping from one hand to the other.

Here you are looking at the magician's hands.

The movement of your hands hides the slight.

Swing your hands back and forth, doing the slight each time.

The thimble seems to have jumped to your other hand.

1 Thumb palm a thimble in your left hand. The other is on your right first finger. Hold both hands at waist level, pointing down and right.

2 Swing your hands to the left, Thumb Palming the thimble on your right finger and retrieving the other with your left first finger as you move.

3 Straighten your fingers as your hands stop. You now have a thimble on your left first finger and one Thumb Palmed in your right hand.

4 Swing your hands back to the right, Palming the thimble on your left hand and retrieving the one in your right.

CABARET MAGIC

In cabaret, an interesting presentation is as important as technical skill. On the next four pages are some well-known cabaret tricks. Do them all, select those you particularly enjoy and try to think of your own way of presenting them.

Afghan Bands

In this trick, three seemingly identical loops of paper are cut in the same way, with odd results. You need three strips of paper 1-2ins wide and 39ins long; glue and scissors.

To prepare the first strip, put a dab of glue on one end of it. Bring the other end round and stick it flat on the gluey bit to make a loop.

Do it again with the second strip, only this time twist the band once by turning your hand before you stick it down.

Repeat with the third band, but this time twist the end twice before you stick it down flat.

Cut each ring in half along its length. Push the point of the scissors through the middle of the band then cut all the way round as shown here by the dotted line.

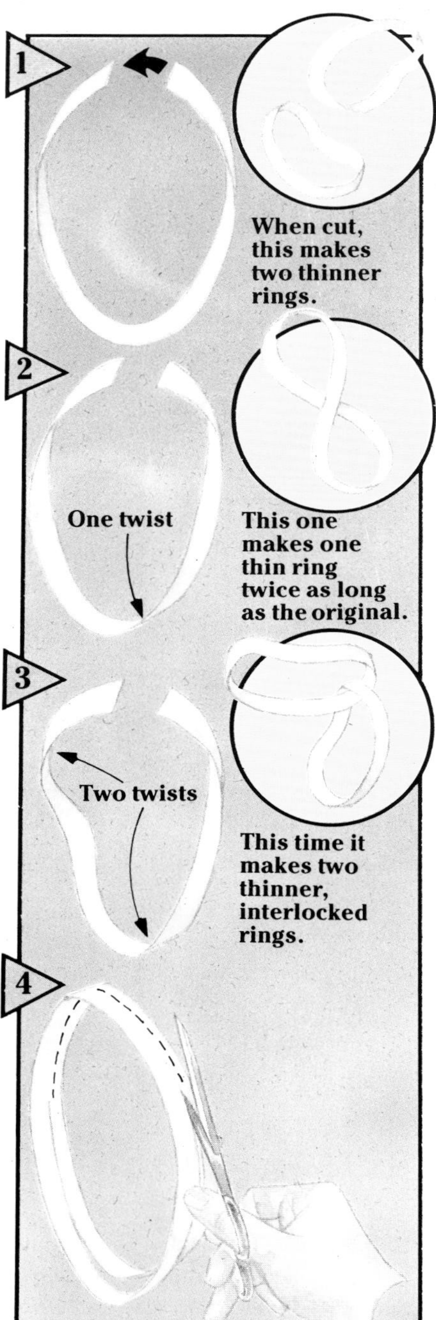

When cut, this makes two thinner rings.

This one makes one thin ring twice as long as the original.

This time it makes two thinner, interlocked rings.

Presentation ideas

Take a theme of wedding rings. Write the names of couples in the audience on each band. Cut between the names. Make joking remarks about the couples according to how the rings turn out. You could say the linked rings showed a very close couple, for example. Don't say anything rude or unpleasant.

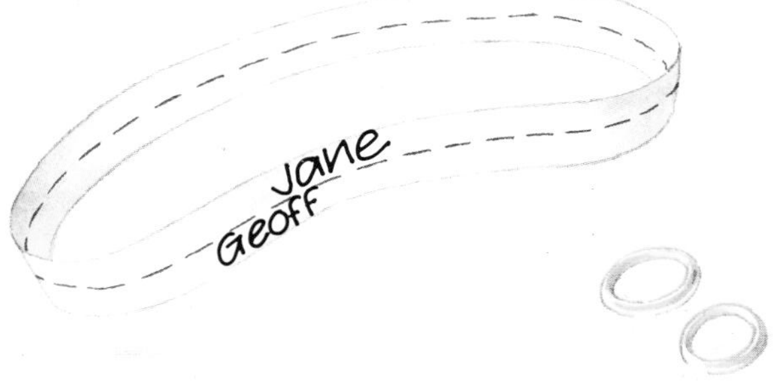

Or start by saying you need more rings for this trick and ask a volunteer to help you cut them. Tell her to copy you exactly. You cut two straight rings, but give her two twisted ones. You can make a joke when her rings don't turn out right.

Cabaret tips

- *Display props at waist height or higher and make sure they can be seen by the whole audience.*
- *Avoid tricks that must be seen from one angle only.*
- *If you put a prop on a table, ensure people can see it all the time or they may suspect you of switching (changing the prop for another that looks identical).*

Cut and Restored Rope

For this trick you will need a piece of rope about 4ft long and a sharp pair of scissors. In magic shops, you can buy special rope that cuts easily, but you can use ordinary rope.

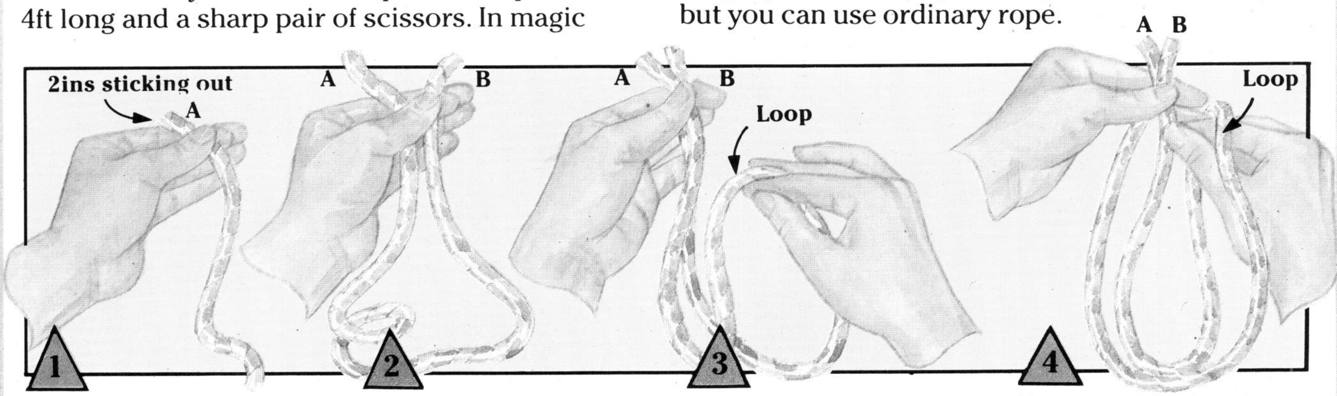

2ins sticking out

1 Take hold of the rope between your left finger and thumb near one end (called A in the picture).

2 Pick up the other end (B) and place it next to A, sticking up by the same amount above your left hand.

3 Take the bottom of the rope loop with your first and second right fingers. Lift it up towards the ends in your left hand.

4 Put your right thumb through the loop and grab end B just below your left thumb.

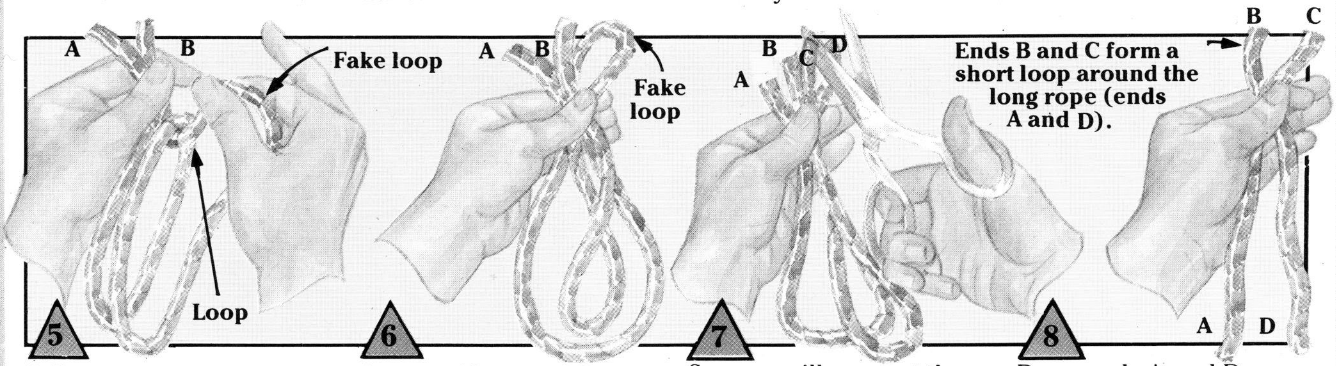

5 Pull some rope up through the loop with your right first finger and thumb to make a fake loop.

6 Let go with your right hand as you take the base of the fake loop in your left hand. Hide the join with your thumb.

7 Say you will now cut the rope. Cut the fake loop. Now you have four ends, A,B,C and D sticking out above your left thumb.

Ends B and C form a short loop around the long rope (ends A and D).

8 Drop ends A and D. (When you practice, you may need to look under your left thumb to check which end is which.)

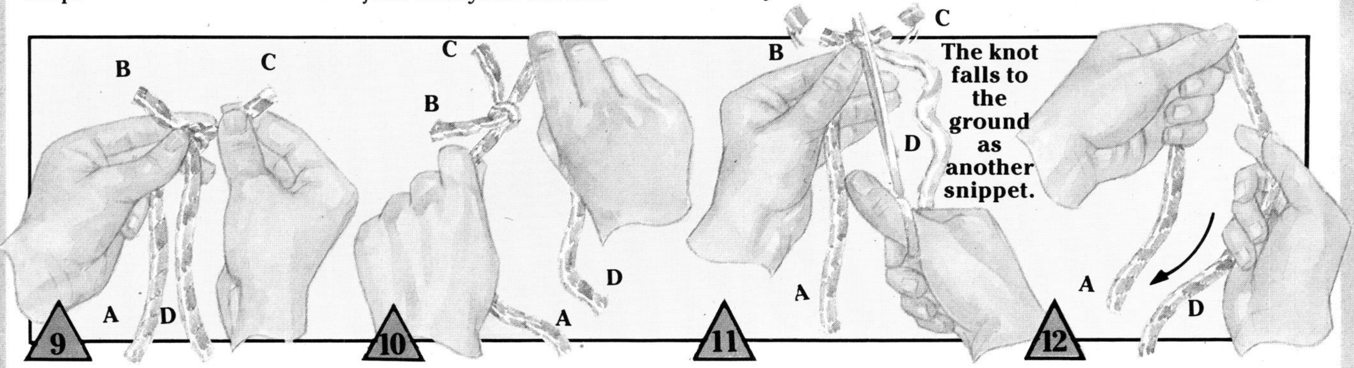

9 You now seem to have two pieces of rope. Say you will make them one again and tie a single knot with ends B and C.

10 Display the knotted rope. People should laugh at this phoney magic. Say you will get rid of the knot.

The knot falls to the ground as another snippet.

11 Hide the knot with your left hand. Snip bits off the short ends and let them fall. Then snip the knot itself off the rope.

12 Take end D in your right hand and slowly pull the rope out of your left hand to show it restored.

Coin in Wool

For this trick you need some wool, a tumbler glass and a cardboard tube, which you can make yourself. See how to prepare the trick on the right. Then follow steps 1 to 6, below, to see how to present it. It helps if your glass is lightly coloured, or patterned, so it is not so easy to see through.

Leave this end open.

3ins.

1.25ins.

Totally cover this end.

▲ Take a piece of thin cardboard about 3ins by 1.25ins Bend the two short sides round to meet each other.

▲ Overlap the short ends by about 0.5ins and stick with glue or tape. Paint it to match the wool you use.

▲ Hold the tube on your finger. Wind wool round it until it looks like a ball. Don't wind it too tightly.

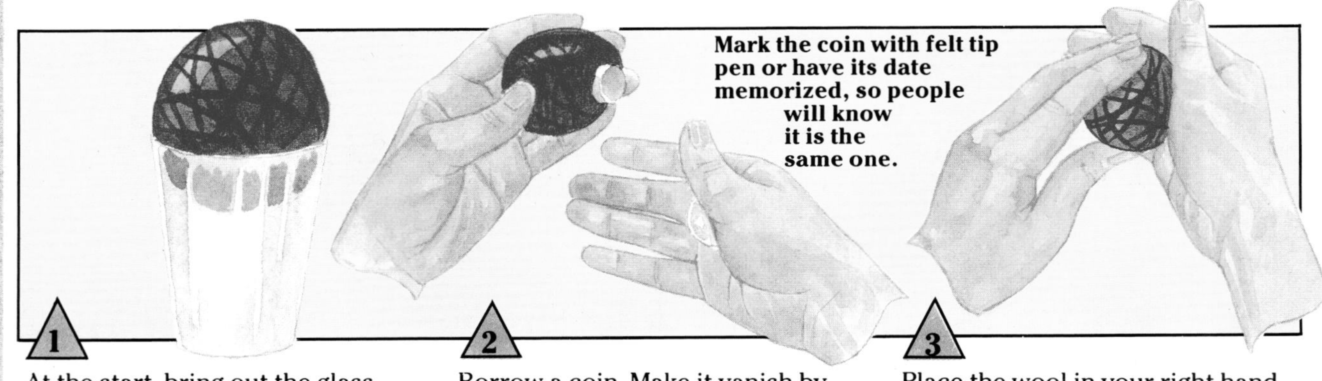

Mark the coin with felt tip pen or have its date memorized, so people will know it is the same one.
1
2
3

1. At the start, bring out the glass with the wool on top. The open end of the tube sticks down into the glass so the audience will not see it.

2. Borrow a coin. Make it vanish by doing a Thumb Palm Vanish (or use the Hankie Vanish on the right). Pick up the wool with your left hand.

3. Place the wool in your right hand, putting the open end of the tube directly over the palmed coin. This frees your left hand to lift the glass.

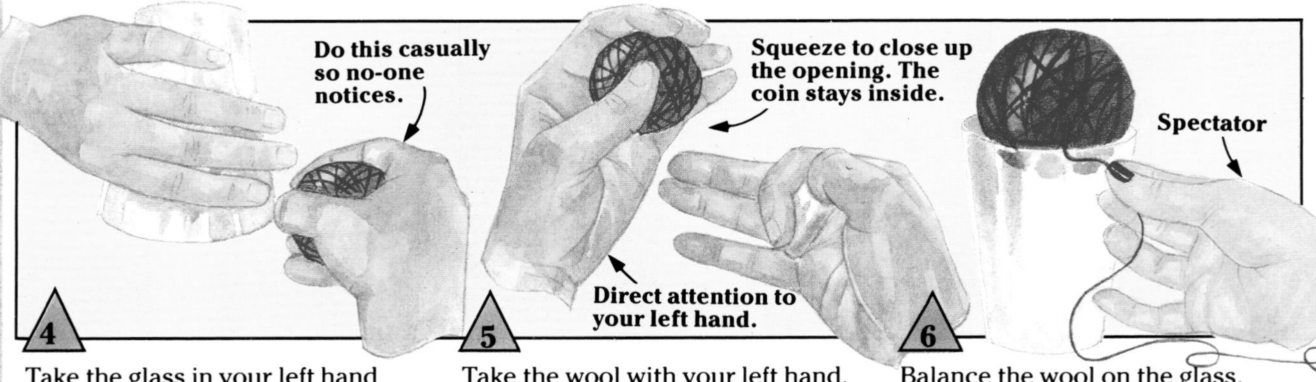

Do this casually so no-one notices.
Squeeze to close up the opening. The coin stays inside.
Spectator
Direct attention to your left hand.
4
5
6

4. Take the glass in your left hand and turn it over to show it is empty. At the same time, turn your right hand over so the coin drops into the tube.

5. Take the wool with your left hand. As you do so, stick your right thumb in the tube, pull it out of the wool and Thumb Palm it in your right hand.

6. Balance the wool on the glass. Hand the end to the person who gave you the coin to pull gently. As the wool unwinds, the coin drops into the glass.

Hankie Vanish

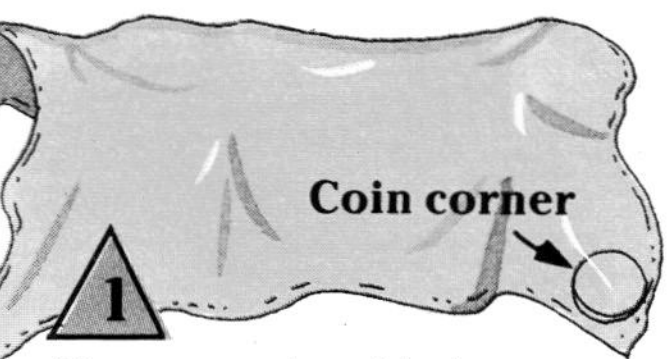

Prepare a hankie by opening the hem at one corner and inserting a small coin. Then sew it up again.

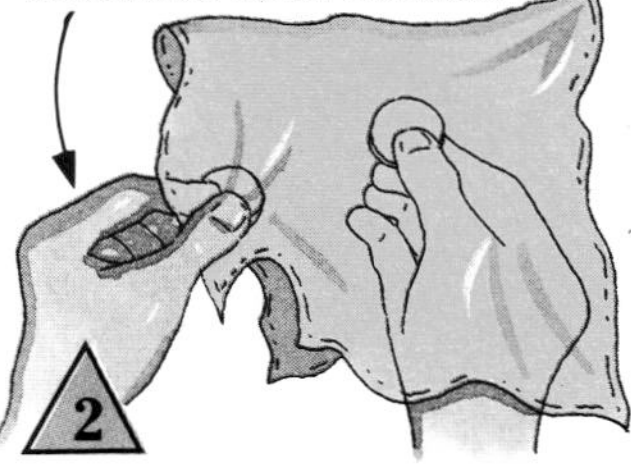

Hold the coin corner.
2

To do the Vanish, take a similar coin in your right hand. With your left hand, drape the hankie over it.

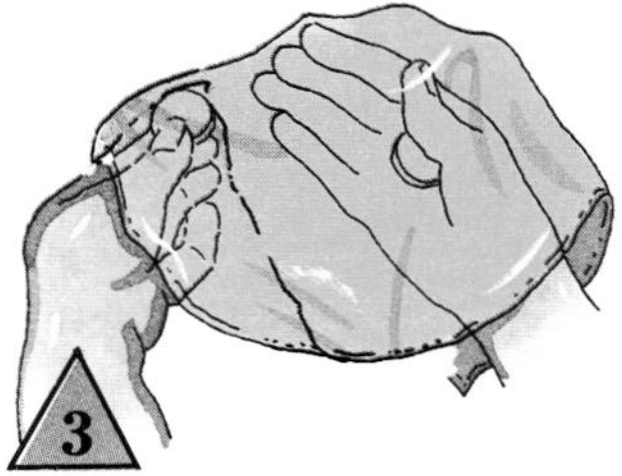

Take the coin corner up underneath into the center of the hankie. Thumb Palm the real coin in your right hand.

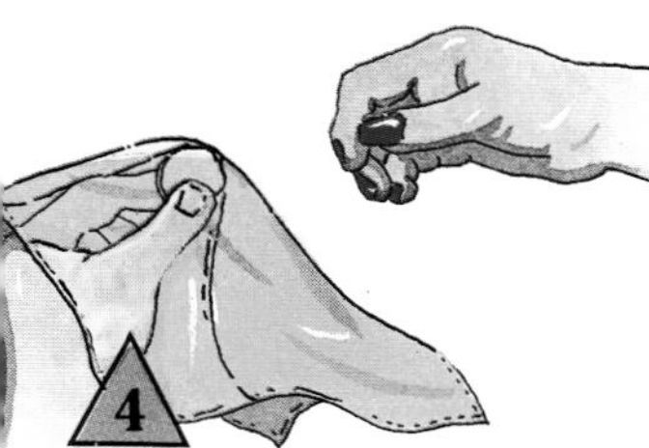

Ask someone to hold the sewn-in coin through the hankie. When you whisk the hankie from him, the coin vanishes.

Two Card Trick

You need a box deep enough to turn cards over in without being seen, and two decks of cards.

To prepare the trick, choose two contrasting cards, such as the two of diamonds (2D) and the ten of spades (10S). Take both cards out of both decks. Take the two cards from one of the decks and stick them back to back. This is called a "double-facer".

Start with the double-facer in your right pocket, with the 10S facing away from you. Openly take the 10S and 2D from the complete pack and put them in the box on a table.

Explain that you will put a card in your pocket (do it with the 10S to show them) and they must guess which card is left. Now bring out the double-facer, showing the 10S.

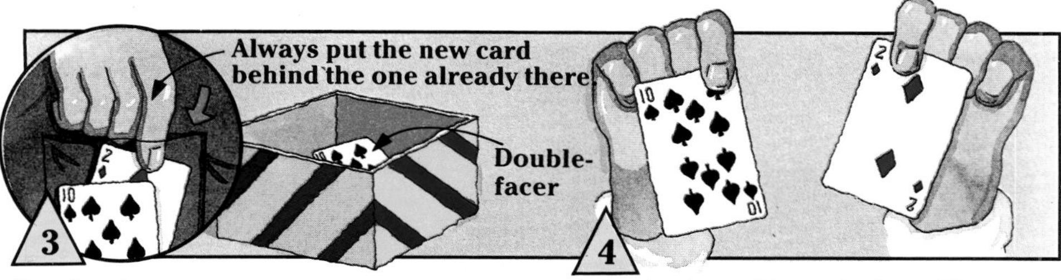

Put the double-facer (10S side up) in the box and say that now you will start for real. Take the 2D from the box, show it briefly and put it in your pocket.

Ask which card is in the box. They will say the 10S. In the box, turn the double-facer to the 2D side then show it to the audience. Take the 10S from your pocket.

Do it slower this time.
5

6

Say you will try again. Put both cards in the box. Turn the double-facer, show its 10S side and put it in your pocket. They will be sure the 2D is left.

Slowly reach in the box and take out the 10S. Then take the 2D from your pocket. Throw both cards in the box and hand it out for inspection.

Presentation tips

- *When you put a card in your pocket always put it behind the one already there. This way, you always know which is which.*
- *Although you use a fake (the double-facer), the cards can be examined at the end as it is hidden in your pocket.*

MENTALISM

Mentalists pretend to use mind-reading, telepathy (sending thoughts from one person to another) and other mental powers. You need confidence to do tricks like these and it helps to have a good memory and a knack for quick thinking.

Specialists

Most specialists like to imply that their powers are real, but are careful not to claim they can definitely predict the future.

They tend not to mix other kinds of tricks in their act.

Slapstick humour does not seem appropriate. Subtle humour may be used.

Some cultivate unusual looks or behavior that will get them noticed.

Book Test

For this trick you need a few books. Then follow these steps:

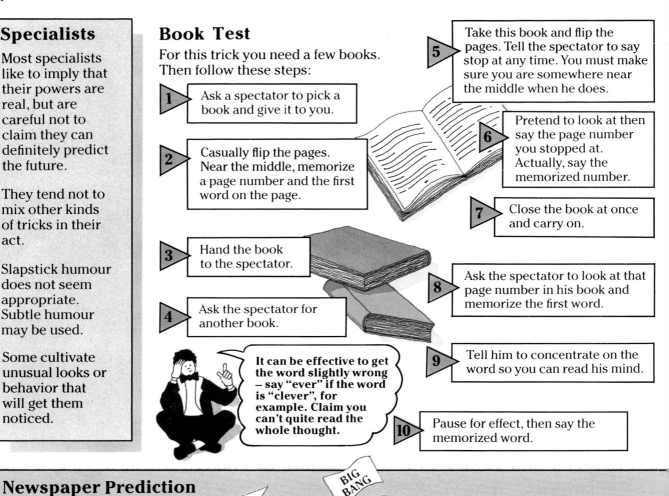

1. Ask a spectator to pick a book and give it to you.
2. Casually flip the pages. Near the middle, memorize a page number and the first word on the page.
3. Hand the book to the spectator.
4. Ask the spectator for another book.
5. Take this book and flip the pages. Tell the spectator to say stop at any time. You must make sure you are somewhere near the middle when he does.
6. Pretend to look at then say the page number you stopped at. Actually, say the memorized number.
7. Close the book at once and carry on.
8. Ask the spectator to look at that page number in his book and memorize the first word.
9. Tell him to concentrate on the word so you can read his mind.
10. Pause for effect, then say the memorized word.

It can be effective to get the word slightly wrong – say "ever" if the word is "clever", for example. Claim you can't quite read the whole thought.

Newspaper Prediction

In this trick, you "predict" where a spectator will tell you to cut a newspaper column. The spectator seems to have a free choice, but you arrange things as described in steps 1 to 3 first. Steps 4 to 7 explain how to present the trick. The column must all be in the same type size, except for the headline.

BIG BANG
BIG BANG
It is best if there is something different on the other side.
People will not be close enough to see the join.
BIG BANG
The line you write is here.

1. Cut a column from the day's newspaper. It should have a headline big enough to read from a distance.
2. Cut off the headline. Cut the top and bottom off the column and turn it upside-down. Stick the headline back on to it.
3. Write out the line of type furthest from the headline. This is your "prediction". Put it in a sealed envelope.

Personality Probe

The method for this trick is simple. It needs good misdirection and a confident presentation to succeed. Some hints are given below.

Don't take more than 10 names.
The audience must not see the names.
Napoleon

1. Take a pad and pen. Ask people to call out the names of famous people. Pretend to write each name on a new page, tear it off and put it on the table.

2. Really, write the first name given on each sheet. To misdirect, ask someone to repeat a name, as if you did not hear it. Ask another to spell a tricky name.

3. Now say you will make a prediction. Write the first name on another sheet of paper. Put this sheet in an envelope and seal it. Give it to a spectator to hold.

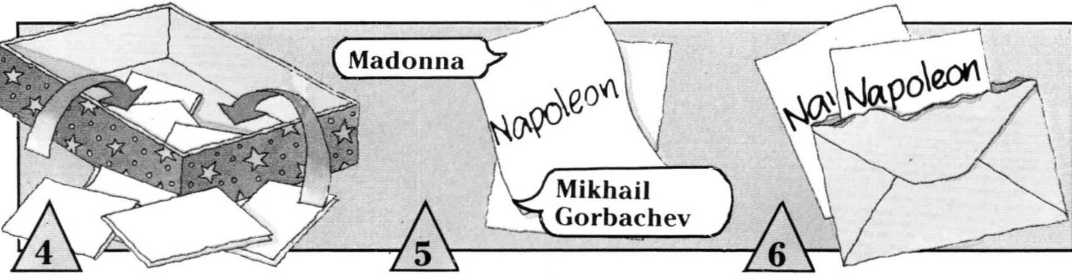

4. Fold all the bits of paper you have written on and put them in a box. Shake them around then get another spectator to pick one out. Place the box aside.

5. Take one or two papers from the box and pretend to read names that were called out earlier. This should convince people that the papers are genuine.

6. Ask the spectator who picked a paper to read the name on it and the one with the envelope to open it and read your prediction. The names are the same.

Tips on mentalism

One or two mentalist tricks can be very effective in any act. Here are some hints about including them:

- *Don't talk about a trick. Say "test" or "experiment".*
- *Be slightly wrong now and then. A guess which is close but not quite right adds authenticity.*
- *If a coincidence or unusual thing happens, claim you planned it.*
- *You will find certain things are likely, such as that people often say 3 if asked for a number between 1 and 5, for example.*
- *Invent scientific "facts" about your powers. They don't have to be true.*

BIG BANG
Memorize a couple of sentences if you cannot read upside-down.
The audience assumes the column is the right way up.
BIG BANG
Let the cut paper fall to the floor.
When it is the right way up, the top line is the one you copied out.

4. Have some scissors ready. Hold up the column and read a bit aloud. Give a spectator the prediction to hold.

5. Say you will run the scissors up and down the column and cut wherever a chosen spectator says stop.

6. Do it, then hand the cut piece to the spectator and ask him to read the top line. He will turn it the right way up.

7. Ask the spectator holding your prediction to open it and read it out. It will be exactly the same line.

CHILDREN'S MAGIC

This kind of magic is usually performed for children of about four to eight years old. It is often part of a birthday party.

Joking, having lots of fun and letting the children join in are more important than doing complicated tricks.

Hello Routine

This is not a trick, but should get you off to a good start. The children get to know you and get used to joining in.

At the start say,

I'm rather shy so would you please say hello when I say hello to you?

Walk away, then come back. Someone is bound to shout hello. Say,

No, no that's wrong. Wait until I say hello first.

Go off and come back again. There should be silence. Wait a bit, then start to look ill at ease. They expect you to speak. You say,

Sorry, I've forgotton what I'm supposed to say.

They will almost certainly shout hello, to remind you. Look relieved and say,

Thank you.

Then go off and come back, saying,

Hello.

You should get a very loud hello in return.

Farmyard Noises

For this trick you need to make six cards, as shown here. They all have the same back (a farm, say) except one. This is a double-facer with a duplicate cow on one side and horse on the other. Pile the cards face-up in the above order (horse on the top, question mark on the bottom). Pin the cow card to your back.

Square the cards and hold them up showing the horse. Ask the children what noise a horse makes and tell them to make it.

Put the horse card at the back and show the pig. Ask them to make the right noise. Put it at the back. Do the same with the sheep.

3

Now introduce the cow as Daisy. Say she's shy and will turn her back. Do a Double Lift (page 34) and turn Daisy and the question mark around.

4

Turn the top card over, showing the question mark. Say it seems that Daisy has gone. Ask the children where she could be.

5

Start to look round for her. Ask the children to help. When you turn your back they will see the other Daisy and will shout out.

6

Pretend not to understand. Turn around comically, looking. Eventually, "realize" what they are saying and "find" the card.

Colorful Silks

You need four silk scarves: two medium sized ones (one red and one yellow); a small one and a big one, both half red and half yellow. You also need a colorful tube, open at both ends, to put them in.

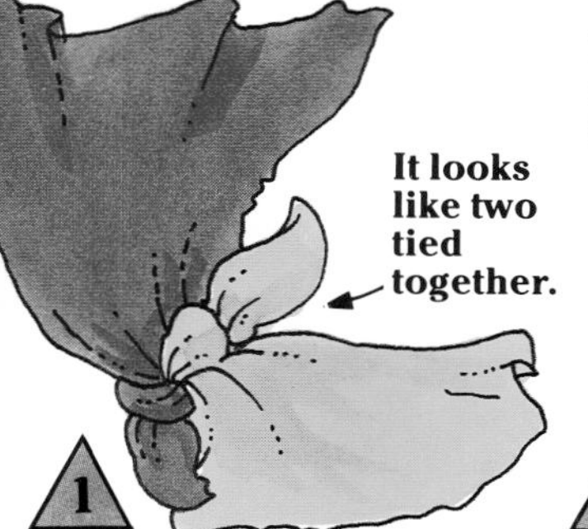

It looks like two tied together.
1

To prepare the trick, tie the small silk round the big silk where the two colors meet. Use a loose single knot.

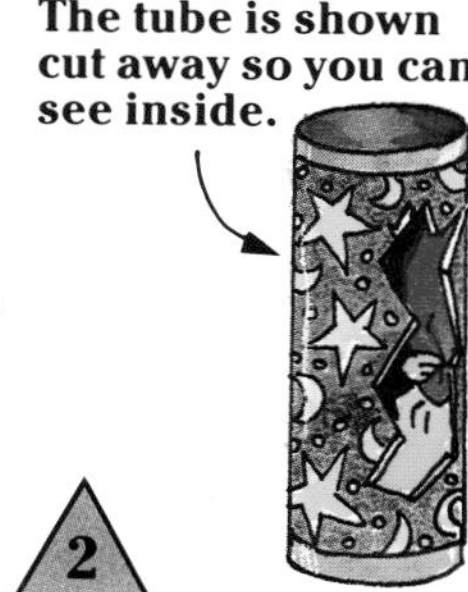

The tube is shown cut away so you can see inside.
2

Hide the knotted silks in the tube, red half near one end and yellow half near the other. You are now ready.

To prepare, tie the small silk round the big one where the colors on the big silk meet. Use a loose, single knot.

Stuff the medium silks into the tube, the same way as the hidden silk (the same colors towards the same ends.)

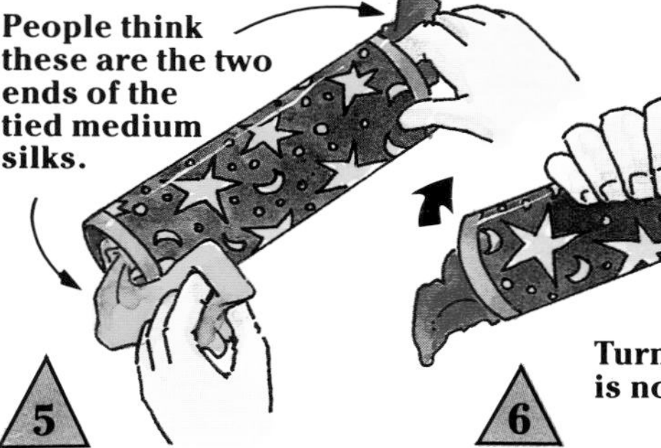

People think these are the two ends of the tied medium silks.
5

As you do, push the hidden silk down and pull out its yellow corner. Leave some red showing at the top.

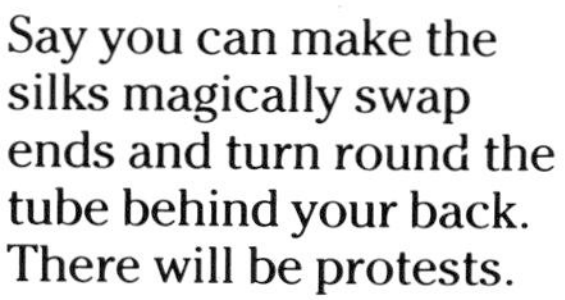

Turning the tube is not magical.
6

Say you can make the silks magically swap ends and turn round the tube behind your back. There will be protests.

Say you will do another trick. Push the red end into the tube and pull the yellow end to remove the big silk.

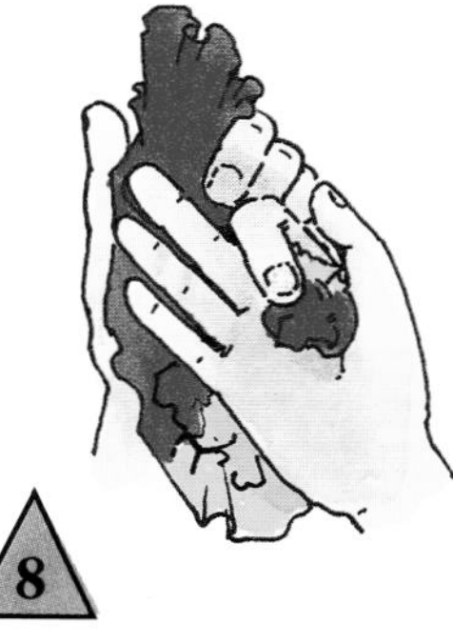

Rumple it up into your left hand. As you do so, secretly undo the small silk and palm it in your right hand.

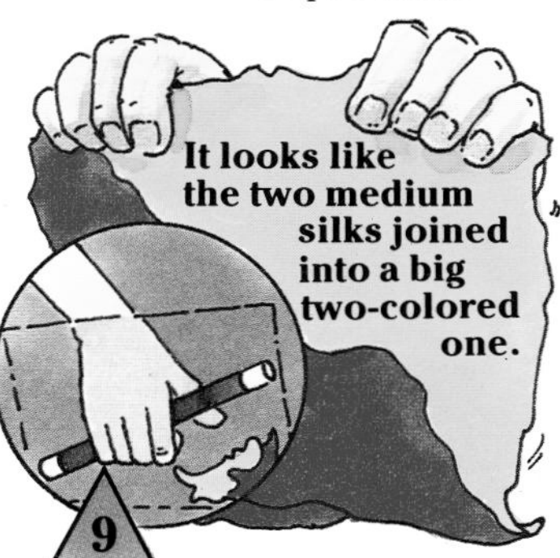

It looks like the two medium silks joined into a big two-colored one.
9

Fetch a wand from your pocket with your right hand. Leave the palmed silk there. Wave the wand and open the big silk.

Magic word book

Take a slim notebook. Write a magic word such as Abracadabra on each page.

On one page attach a cardboard cut-out of a wizard, as below.

Make holes.
Fix elastic to the other side of the wizard and stick the other end on the page.
Paper fastener

Put fastener through holes in corner of wizard and paper. Flatten prongs.

Now when you search for a magic word, push the wizard sideways out of the book with your thumb.

Pretend not to notice. The children will shout out. Release the wizard and the elastic pulls him back in.

Make out you don't know what the children are talking about. This can be a running gag through your act.

Handy hint

Don't let children get over excited. It helps to make them sit down so they can't dash forward at any excuse.

ESCAPOLOGY

Not many magicians specialize in escapology. It is more often used as a publicity stunt or as one part of an act. Spectacular escapes are often dangerous and should only be attempted by experienced professionals.

Sack Escape

For this escape you need a big canvas sack with eyelets around the top, through which to thread a rope, and an assistant to put up a screen.*

1 Pick a volunteer. Climb into the sack. As you crouch down, pull down inside with you a loop of rope about 13ins long.

2 Ask the volunteer to tie the rope securely. You must hold the loop tightly.

3 Have the screen put in front of you. Let go of the loop and you have room to get your hands out to undo the knots and escape.

The thicker the rope, the harder it is to tie tightly.

Never use a plastic bag or sack in this trick.

Tips on escapology

- *Rehearse in harder conditions than necessary, with help nearby. Then you should be able to cope if things go wrong on stage.*
- *Check props rigorously.*
- *Brief helpers with extra care.*
- *Make it look harder than it is. Expend lots of energy; wince and groan as if it hurts.*

Rope Escape

This escape requires a scarf or handkerchief, a rope and a volunteer. On stage, you might use a screen, but it works just as well using a jacket to hide your hands.

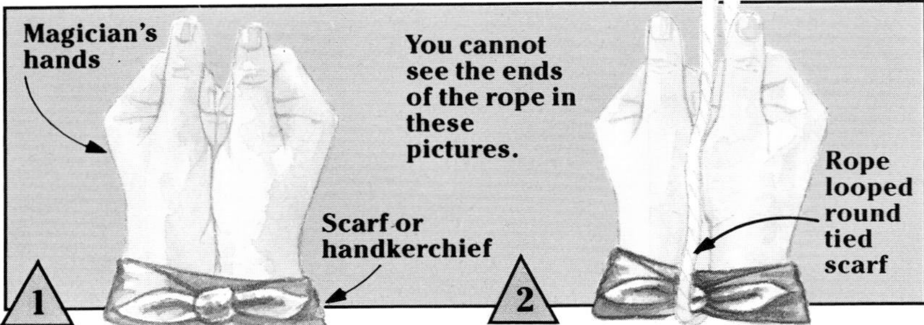

You cannot see the ends of the rope in these pictures.

Rope looped round tied scarf

1 Have your wrists tied. Try to get room to manouvre by twisting your wrists so they are not quite flat together.

2 Get a volunteer to put the rope between your arms and hold both ends. Make him move away from you a bit.

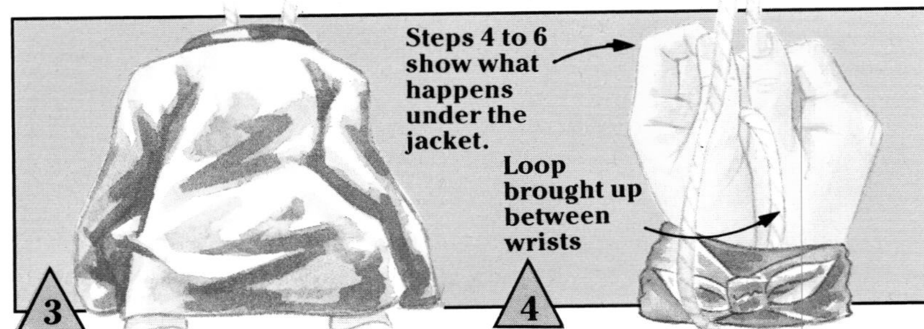

Steps 4 to 6 show what happens under the jacket.
Loop brought up between wrists
3
4

3 Have a jacket thrown over your hands. The helper still holds the rope ends. (With a screen, the helper stays in front.)

4 Wriggle your wrists to bring the loop of rope that is between your arms up through the tied scarf and between your wrists.

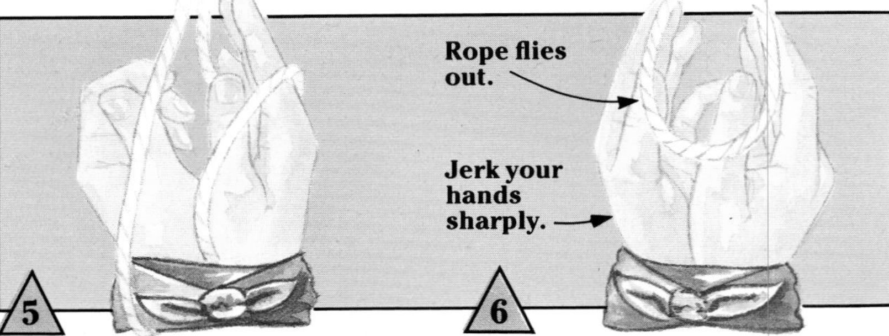

Rope flies out.

5 As quickly as you can, work the loop up and over one hand. Let it fall slack to the outside.

6 Now jerk your hands back. The rope slips out under the handkerchief and you escape. Your hands are still tied.

Make absolutely sure your assistant knows the signal you will give if you are in trouble.

Illusions are exciting to perform but the cost of equipment, the difficulty of transporting it, caring for live animals and the need to employ assistants are all potential problems. It can even be hard to find venues to perform some big illusions.

Pushmi-Pullu

This illusion does not involve buying anything except a rope. You do, however, need two people to help you and a stage to perform on. The stage must have wings on each side (areas to walk off into, out of sight of the audience) and a means of getting from one side to the other without being seen. Your acting skills are also important to make it look effective.

One assistant is in the wings holding the rope. You walk on stage from this side, dragging the rope over your shoulder as if you are pulling a heavy weight on the end.

Go across the stage and off the other side. Give the second assistant the rope to keep pulling so it looks as if you carry on walking. Run unseen back to the first side.

Take the end of the rope from the first assistant and let the second pull you on stage. This gives the illusion that the heavy weight you were pulling was yourself.

Lean back against the pull of the rope to make it as realistic as you can. Let yourself be pulled off the other side before returning to take a bow.

Tips on illusions

- *Most illusions must be bought from a magic dealer or specially made.*
- *Learn to handle all parts of the illusion smoothly.*
- *Don't let the preparation drag.*
- *Costumes, scenery, props and lighting should be carefully thought out to enhance the effect.*
- *Try to ensure that the audience thinks you, rather than the prop, are responsible for the illusion.*

QUICK EFFECTS

The effects on these two pages are most startling done casually. Don't build them up as big tricks but do them in passing, when you happen to have the prop to hand.

Jumping Match

1. Hold a safety match tightly near its head end in your left first finger and thumb. Put your second fingernail under it and press down hard against that, too. *

2. Balance a second match on the first, as shown. Let it rest lightly on your right first finger.

It can be hard to get the right effect at first. Keep practicing.

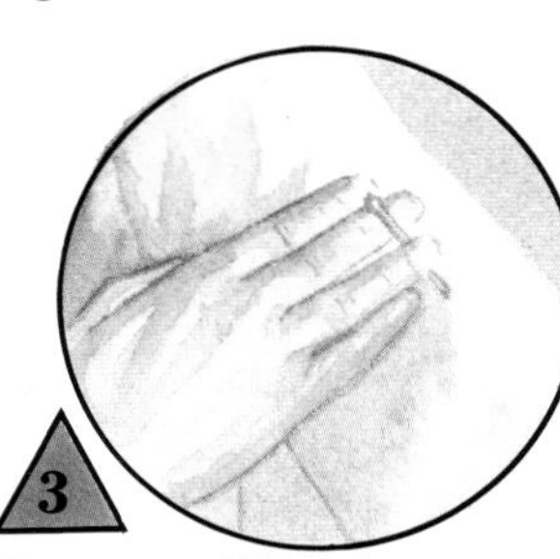

3. Say you will fill the second match with static electricity. Rub it on your sleeve then replace it.

4. Now if you move the first match slightly, the friction against your fingernail causes a twitch making the second match leap.

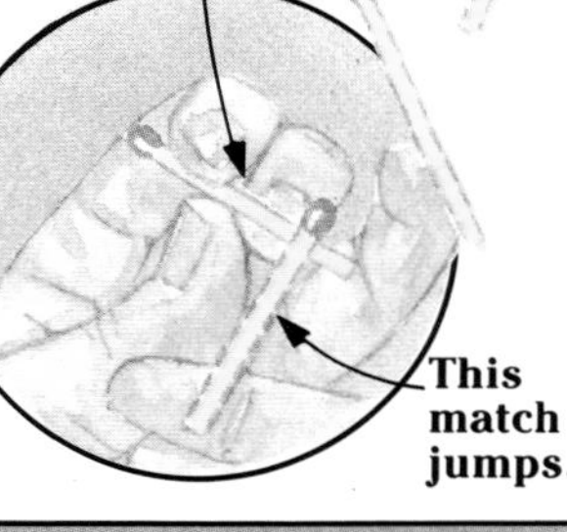

Match rubs against nail.
This match jumps.

Twangy Band

1. Out of sight, put an elastic band over your first two right fingers. Pull it towards you with your left first finger.

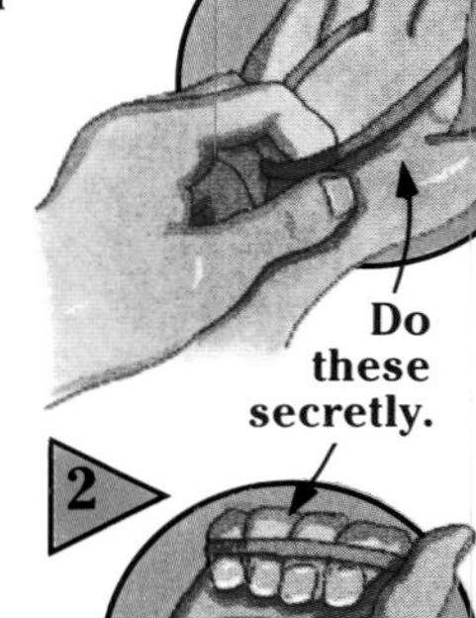

Do these secretly.

2. Curl all your right fingers, put them inside the elastic, then release it so they are all enclosed. Now you are ready.

3. Hold up your fist to show the band round the first two fingers. Uncurl your fingers and it jumps to the third and fourth ones.

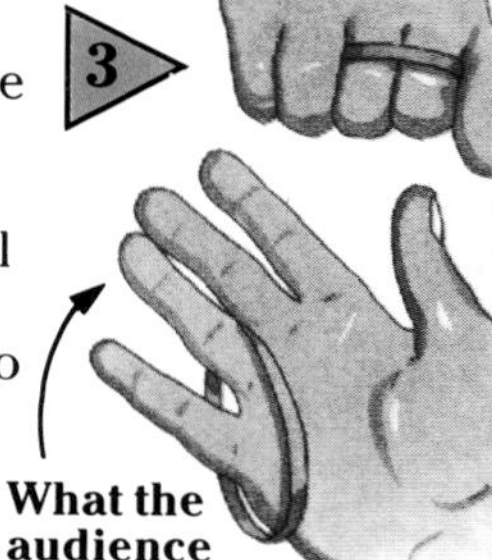

What the audience sees.

Rubber Pencil

Hold the pencil loosely in your first finger and thumb. Twist your wrist rapidly round one way and back the other, making the pencil wag.

This gives the illusion that the pencil bends.

Stretching Silk

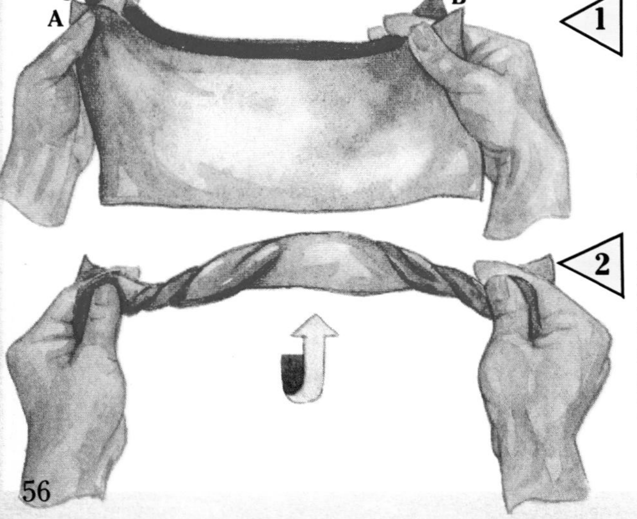

C
A
D
B

1. Fold a silk in two, as shown. Hold corners A and B between your thumbs and first fingers; and hold C and D between your first and second fingers.

2. Make small circles with your hands towards yourself to twirl the silk around itself. You could now consider and say the silk should be a bit longer.

You are now holding the silk diagonally.

3. Let go of corners A and D. Hold onto B and C and keep twirling. Move your hands further apart and the silk seems to stretch.

Dollar Bill Puzzle

You can do this puzzling trick with any bank bill. One with a face or figure on is best as it clearly has a right and wrong way up. You can do it more than once, if you like.

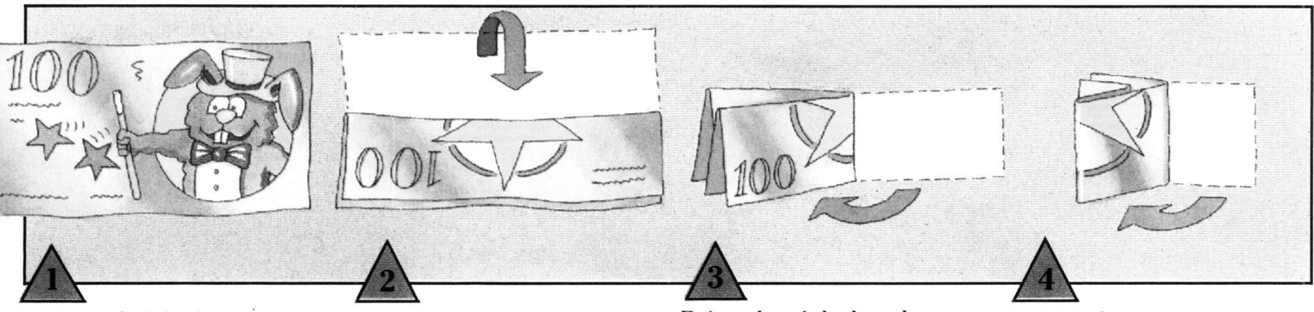

1. Hold the bill facing you. Point out that it is the right way up.

2. Fold it down towards you lengthways.

3. Bring the right hand edges towards you and over onto the left hand edges to fold it in half widthways.

4. Fold it the same way again, taking the right side over to the left.

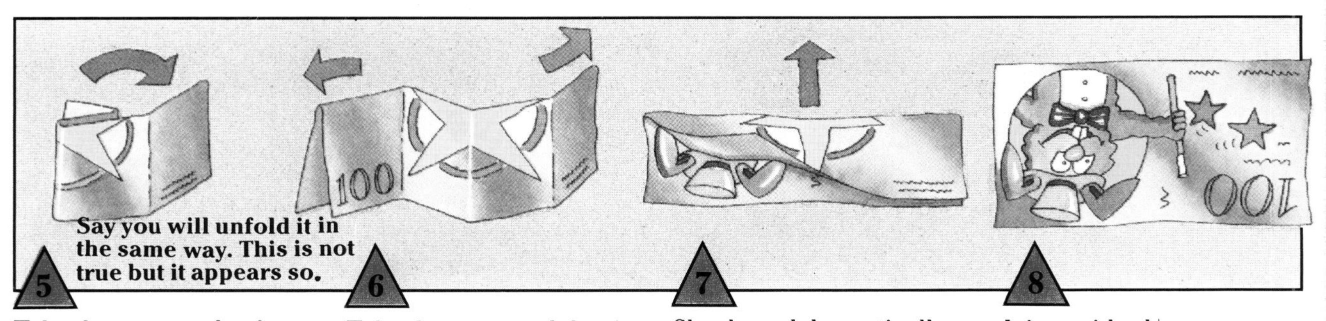

Say you will unfold it in the same way. This is not true but it appears so.

5. Take the open ends of the bill (at the back on the left side) and unfold them away from you and to the right.

6. Take the open end that is now at the back on the right side and unfold it away from you and to the left.

7. Slowly and dramatically, unfold the bill towards you lengthways.

8. It is upside-down, without being turned. If you repeat the trick, do it swiftly so no-one can work it out.

Levitating Matches

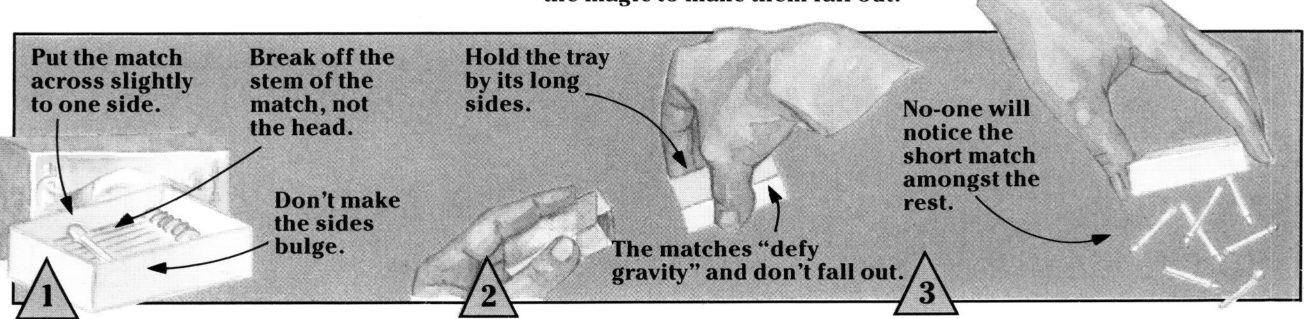

You could say some magic words to make the matches stay in, then "undo" the magic to make them fall out.
Put the match across slightly to one side.
Break off the stem of the match, not the head.
Don't make the sides bulge.
Hold the tray by its long sides.
The matches "defy gravity" and don't fall out.
No-one will notice the short match amongst the rest.

1. Set up a box of matches like this: break the end off one match so it fits the box width exactly. Place it across the other matches, as shown. *

2. Now you can bring out the matchbox and push the drawer half out to show the matches. Then close it, turn it over and push the tray right out.

3. Put the box cover down and take the tray in your free hand. This time hold it by the short sides and squeeze gently. The matches will now drop out.

****Be extra careful when using matches not to light one accidentally.***

PROPS TO MAKE

Many magicians like to make their own props so they can tailor them to their needs. Here are some you could make and some ways to use them.

Production tube

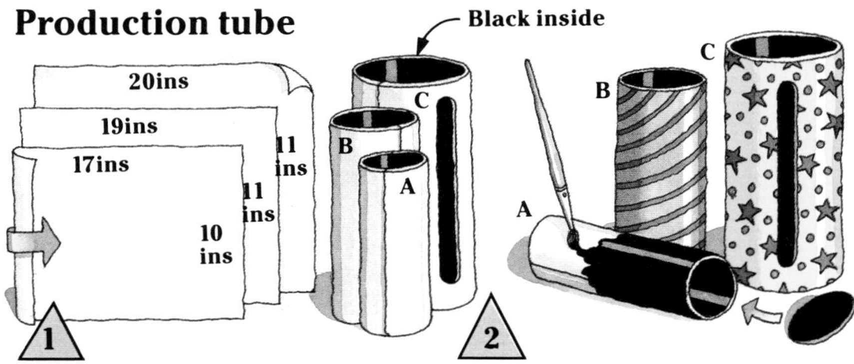

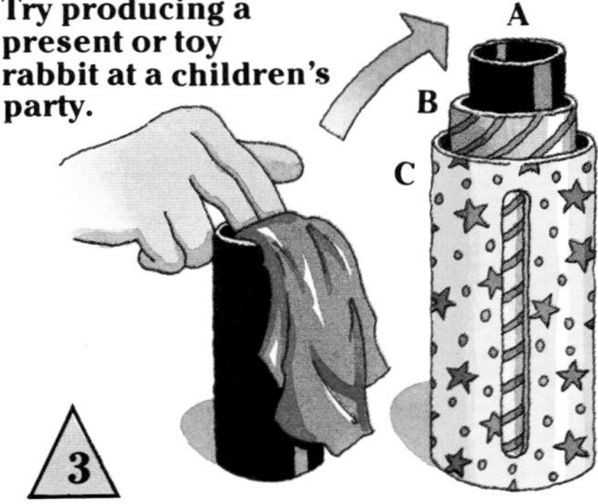

1. You need three pieces of poster board of about these sizes. Paint one side of each black. Then roll them into tubes and stick down.

2. Stick a circle of poster board on tube A as a bottom. Paint A black. Cut a long hole in tube C. Decorate B and C brightly.

3. To prepare a trick, put a prop in tube A then put A in tube B and B in tube C. Have the tubes upright on your table to start.

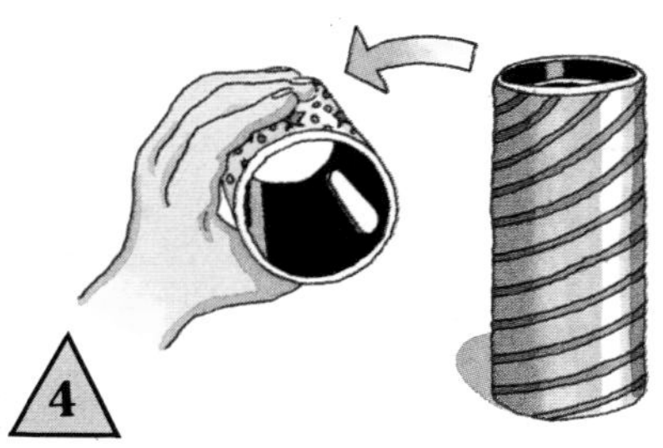

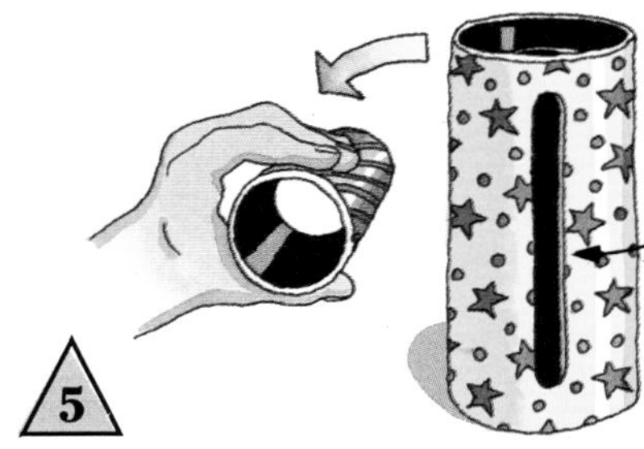

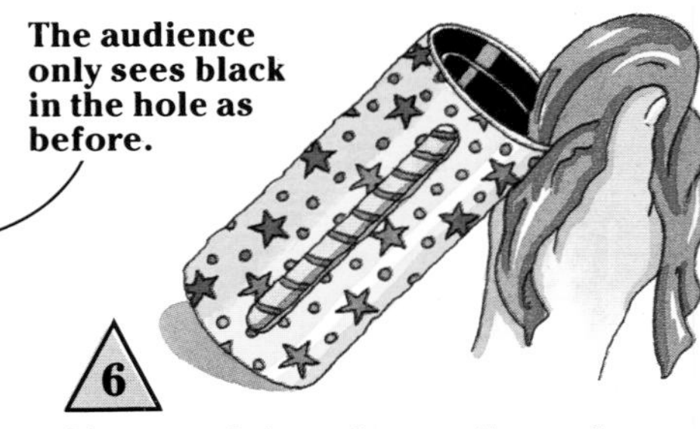

The audience only sees black in the hole as before.

4. Lift tube C off the other two tubes and show the audience it is empty. Then replace it.

5. Draw tube B out from between A and C and show the audience it is empty, too. Now replace it.

6. Now reach into the smallest tube and take your prop out of the "empty" tubes.

Thimble holder

Here is how you can make a holder from which to steal thimbles during an act. Pin it somewhere hidden but within easy reach. Experiment to find the best place.

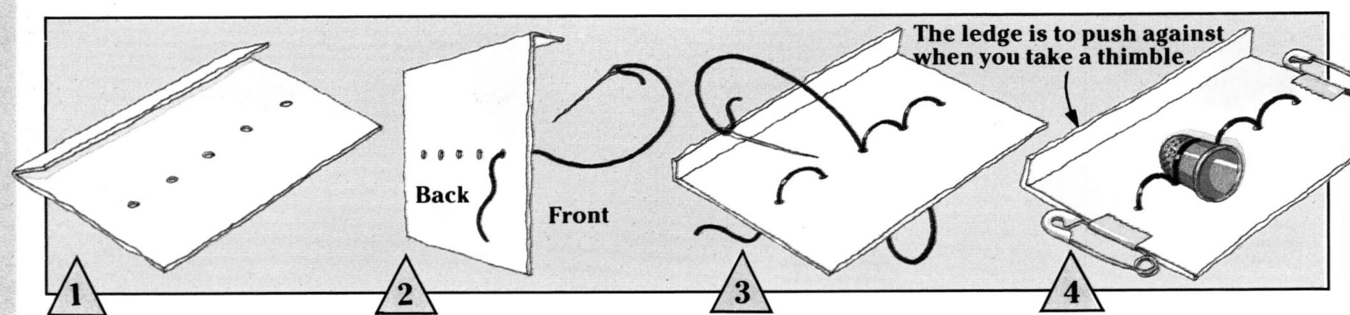

Back
Front
The ledge is to push against when you take a thimble.

1. Take a piece of strong cardboard and bend one long edge over by about 0.5in. Make five evenly-spaced holes in the card.

2. Thread some narrow elastic through the holes. Start at one end and go in and out of consecutive holes.

3. When you reach the far end, come back the other way. Now you have four loops of elastic on your cardboard.

4. Tie the loose ends in a knot. Tape safety pins to each side of the cardboard. The loops will hold four thimbles.

Foxes and Chickens

Here you can see how to make the props to do the Foxes and Chickens trick underneath. The trick makes use of the fact that you can only see three sides of a cube from any angle. You need to make seven small cubes and prepare two larger boxes.

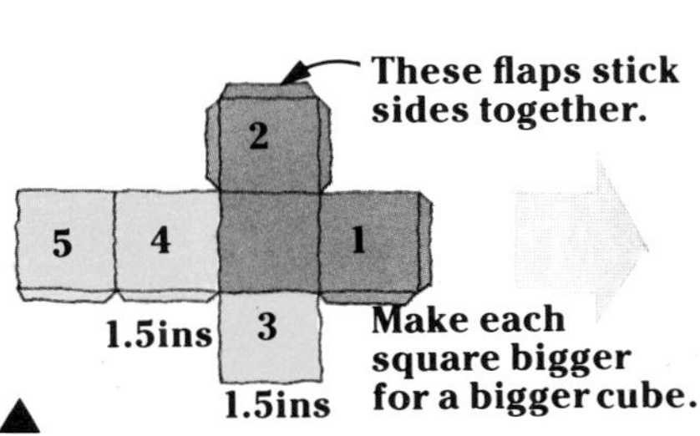

These flaps stick sides together.

Make each square bigger for a bigger cube.

For each cube, draw a shape like this and cut it out. Paint five of them all blue and the other two half blue and half yellow, as shown above.

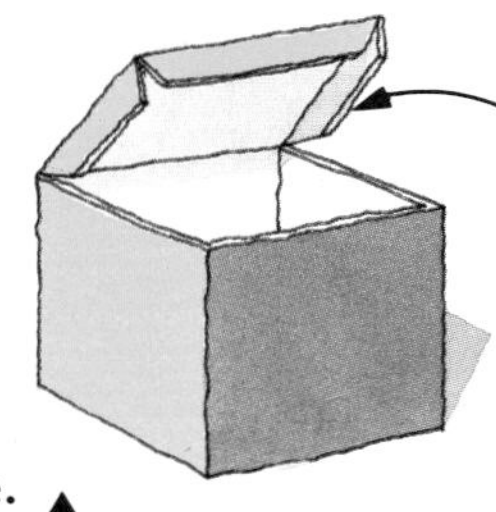

Cubes painted like this can look yellow from one angle and blue from the opposite one.

Fold the flaps up, then fold each square up to make a box, starting with square 1. Glue the flaps inside the adjacent sides to hold it together.

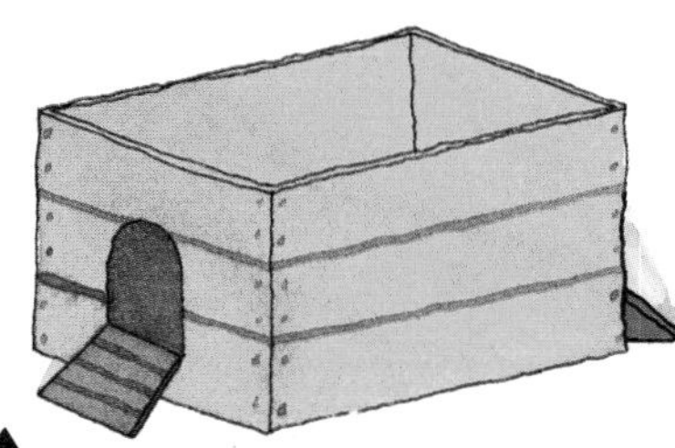

You could paint the bigger boxes like chicken coops. Or just cover them with bright paper or paint.

The trick

The speech bubbles give the story to tell and under the pictures are the moves to make. You see it from the magician's point of view. The two-colored cubes are called YB for short.

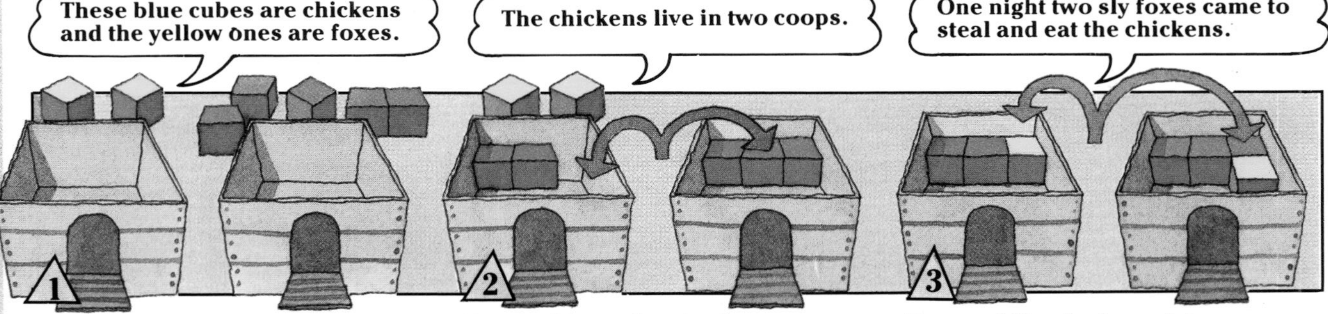

These blue cubes are chickens and the yellow ones are foxes.
The chickens live in two coops.
One night two sly foxes came to steal and eat the chickens.
1
2
3

1. Put the boxes and cubes on a table, showing the yellow sides of the YB cubes.
2. Put the blue cubes in alternate boxes one at a time, starting with the box on your right.
3. Put one YB cube in each box.

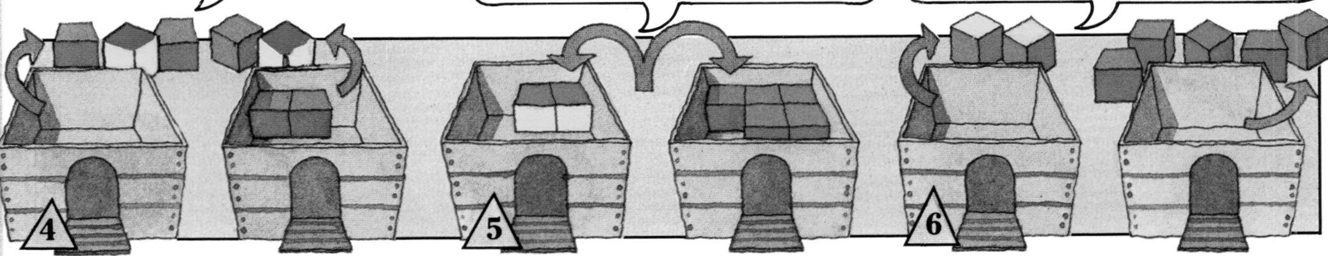

But the chickens heard them coming and ran away.
The foxes hid in the coops and kept quiet so the chickens came back.
It could have been a disaster. But these were very clever chickens. Next day, the farmer found all the chickens in one coop and two foxes trapped in the other.
4
5
6

4. Take five cubes one by one from alternate boxes, starting on your left. Take the YB ones first, turning them to show the blue sides.
5. Put five cubes in the boxes like this: blue to the right, YB to the left, repeat once, then put a blue to the right.
6. Take the cubes out of each box as you speak, showing the yellow side of the YB ones.

See for yourself how versatile magic can be. Try making each of the varied tricks below suit several styles of act. You will find some help on the page opposite.

Thumb Surprise

The audience seems to see one whole thumb.

Your thumb tip seems removeable.

1 Bend both thumbs and fit them together as shown above.

2 Cover the join with the first two fingers of your right hand.

3 Move your right hand away from your left then together again.

Glasses and Bottles

What you need:

Two dark colored plastic bottles (they must not be see-through). Cut their bottoms off with a knife. ▶

▼ Two glasses to fit under the bottles.

▼ Two cardboard tubes to slip over the bottles. They should fit snugly so that when you squeeze gently you can pick the bottle up with the tube (or do it by putting a finger in the top of the bottle).

1 Start with one glass under a bottle and a tube (A) and the second glass under the other bottle, next to the tube (B).

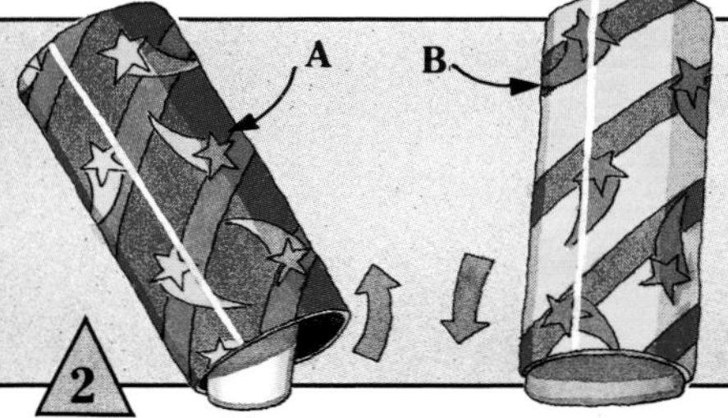

2 Lift up tube A and the bottle to show a glass. Slip tube B over the second bottle. Say you will swap the glass and bottle.

3 Look into both tubes and say that they have swapped. Now say that you will do the hard bit and make them swap back again.

4 Lift tube A and bottle and tube B alone to show the bottle and glass where they were before. No-one will be impressed.

5 Say that as they don't believe you, you will do it again. Lift tube A to show a bottle and tube B and bottle to show a glass.

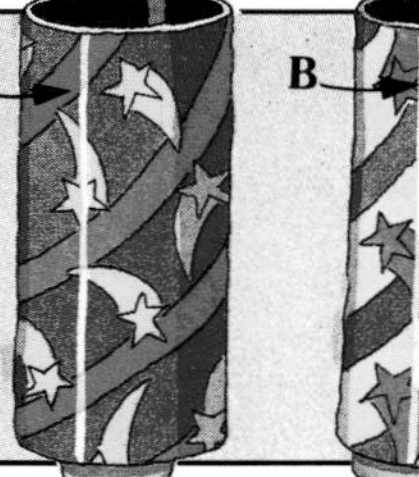

6 Make them swap back again by lifting tube B on its own and tube A and bottle. Make them swap back and forth quite fast.

Bangle on a String

For this trick you need a large ring (a plastic bangle is ideal), 6ft of string and a scarf.

First let spectators look at the ring and string. Don't give them the string for long. Pretend not to want it examined closely, to misdirect suspicion.

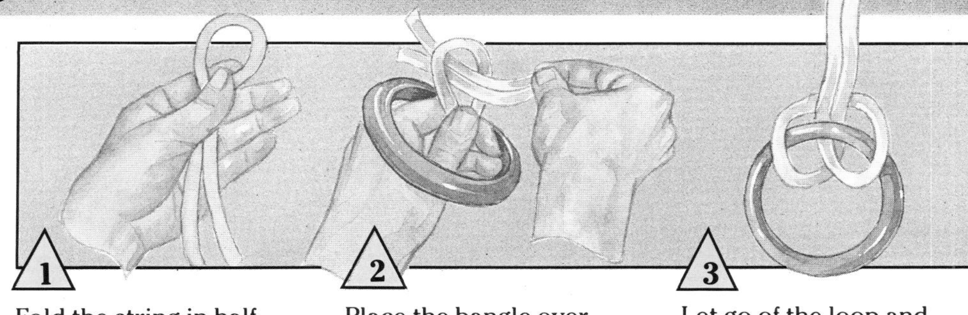

1 Fold the string in half and take hold of it near the loop that is made, as shown.

2 Place the bangle over the loop. Pick up the two loose ends of the string and thread them through the loop.

3 Let go of the loop and pull the ends. This knot will keep the bangle tightly fastened to the string.

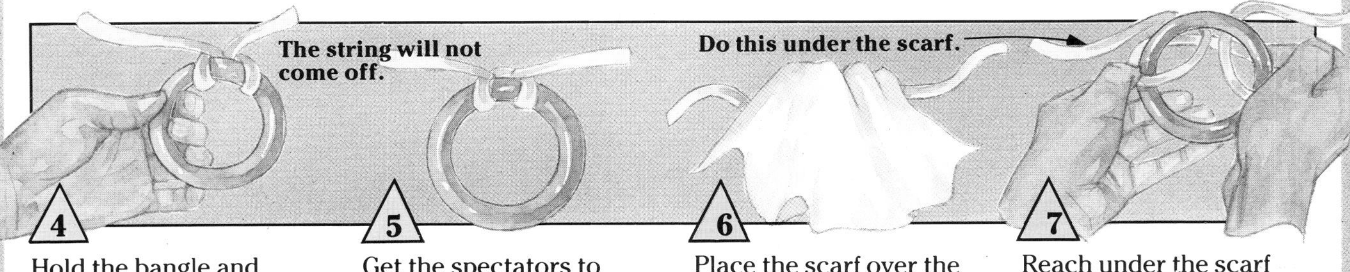

The string will not come off.
Do this under the scarf.

4 Hold the bangle and hand the string ends to two spectators. Ask them to try to pull the string off.

5 Get the spectators to stand on either side of you and pull hard on the string. The bangle remains firmly fixed.

6 Place the scarf over the bangle. Get the helpers to move a bit nearer to you to give you some slack string.

7 Reach under the scarf and slip the loops of the knot round and off the bangle, as shown. Whisk off the scarf.

Pegasus Coin

Use a clean coin.
Be careful not to swallow the coin when you do this.
Pretend to follow the invisible coin with your eyes.
Your left hand is seen empty when you "throw" the coin.

1 Show the audience a coin in each of your hands. Place the coin in your left hand between your lips.

2 Pretend to put the coin in your right hand into your left, but actually French Drop it to leave it in the right hand.

3 Take the coin from your lips with your right fingers. Mime throwing a coin from your left hand into the air.

4 As you mime catching it, drop the coin in your fingers on the one already in your hand and show both.

Variations to try

Thumb Surprise

1. Quick close-up trick.
2. Comedy for children.
3. "Pretend" loosening-up exercise before a trick.

Glasses and Bottles

1. Done silently.
2. Done with patter.
3. Played "straight".
4. Played for laughs.

Bangle on a String

1. Use ring, string and hankie in close-up.
2. Use hoop, rope and coat for cabaret.
3. In escapology act.

Pegasus Coin

1. Close-up trick.
2. Use as quick effect in cabaret, before the Miser's Dream (page 42), for example.

MAGIC INFORMATION

Below is a selection of useful addresses and information to do with magic. You can also extend your magic vocabulary with the list of magic words on page 63.

Books

There are hundreds of books on magic. Look for them in your library or a large bookshop. These ones are especially good in particular areas. You should be able to get them in magic shops, or from Books by Post (see Mail Order, below).

Introductory books

The Magic Book – Harry Lorayne
The Amateur Magician's Handbook – Henry Hay
Classic Secrets of Magic – Bruce Elliott.

History of magic

The Illustrated History of Magic – Milbourne Christopher
The Great Illusionists – Edwin A. Dawes.

Presentation and technique

Our Magic – Nevil Maskelyne and David Devant
Magic and Showmanship – Henning Nelms
Forging Ahead in Magic – John Booth

Advanced and specialist books

The Royal Road to Card Magic and Expert Card Technique – Jean Hugard and Frederick Brauer.
The New Modern Coin Magic – J.B. Bobo.
It's Easier Than You Think – Geoffrey Buckingham (manipulation)
Annemann's Practical Mental Effects – Ted Annemann
Magic with Faucett Ross – Lewis Ganson (cabaret)
The Dai Vernon Book of Magic – Lewis Ganson (close-up and cabaret)
The Tarbell Course in Magic (7 volumes) – Harlan Tarbell (general)

Shops

Magic shops can be found in your local telephone directory under Magicians' Supplies. Many of them sell puzzles and jokes as well as tricks. The following ones cater specifically for magicians.

**Louis Tannen Inc.
6 West 32nd St.
New York
New York 10001**

**Abbott's Magic Company
Colon
Michigan 49040**

Magic conventions

At magic conventions you can buy tricks, watch magic shows and meet other magicians. They are held all over the world and usually last for one or two days. Find out exact dates and details in Genii magazine (see Magazines, right).

Mail order

Many companies sell props by mail. They advertize in Genii (see right). For information on mail orders, send a stamped, self-addressed envelope to:

Louis Tannen, Inc., 6 West 32nd St. NY, NY, 0001, *or* Abbott's Magic Company, Colon, Michigan 49040

Magazines

Here are some magic magazines that you can subscribe to or buy in magic shops. Genii is a monthly publication and contains news, reviews and tricks. Its address is:

**Genii International
Conjuror's Magazine
P.O. Box 3608
Los Angeles
CA 90036**

The Supreme Magic Company, 64, High Street, Bideford, Devon EX 39 2AN, England.

Magic Societies

There are many magic clubs and societies. Enquire at local magic shops (see left) to find ones in your area. Unfortunately, many clubs have restrictions such as that you must be over 18 or male to join. Two famous international magic societies are:

The Magic Circle

The Magic Circle is a club that only allows men over 18 to join but anyone can seek information from them. To become a member, a magician must perform his act to be judged by other members. He may not be accepted first time but he can try again until he is considered good enough. The Magic Circle meets every Monday evening at present in temporary premises. If you would like to know more about it, write to this address:

The Honorary Secretary,
The Magic Circle,
C/O The Victory Services Club,
63/79 Seymour Street,
London W2 2HE

The International Brotherhood of Magicians

This is an international society with groups or "rings" in each country. The American Ring organizes a four day magic convention in July of each year. The contact address is:

IBM Executive Secretary,
P.O. Box 89,
Bluffton,
Ohio, 45817

Some magic words

Here are some words associated with magic and magicians. You will have seen some of them in the book already. Here you can find out exactly what they mean when magicians use them.

Abracadabra

A word supposed to have magic power. It may come from Latin and has probably been in use since the 17th century.

Conjuror

This originally meant someone who called upon supernatural forces to do amazing things. Now, it is another name for a magician.

Hey Presto

Sometimes said by magicians, usually as they reveal a magic effect. *Presto* is an Italian word meaning "immediately".

Hocus Pocus

Magic words used as a magician does a trick. It is thought that they may date from the 17th century, invented from mock Latin.

Legerdemain

This is a French word that some people use for slight of hand. It literally means "light of hand".

Levitate

To make something lift off the ground or hang in the air with no visible means of support. Levitating a lady is a famous trick.

Phantasmagoria

A word invented in the 19th century to mean a magic show in which "phantasms", or ghosts, appeared.

Prestidigitator

This is a name for a slight of hand artist. It derives from the old French word *preste*, meaning nimble, and the Latin *digitus*, which means finger.

Produce

To make something appear magically. To re-produce is to make something appear again after it has been made to disappear.

Restore

Means to make something that is apparently broken or lost reappear whole and unharmed.

Transpose

To make one thing change places magically with another.

Vanish

Used to describe making something disappear. "The magician vanished a whole deck of cards," for instance.

INDEX

First published in 1989 by Usborne Publishing Ltd, Usborne House, 83-85 Saffron Hill, London EC1N 8RT, ENGLAND.
 Printed in Belgium.
AE